# THE
# PRODUCTIVITY
# ZONE

## A Simple System for Time Management

## MORGAN TYREE

**SPIRE**

© 2019 by Morganize with Me, LLC

Published by Revell
a division of Baker Publishing Group
PO Box 6287, Grand Rapids, MI 49516-6287
www.revellbooks.com

Spire edition published 2023
ISBN 978-0-8007-4256-0 (mass market)
ISBN 978-1-4934-4100-6 (ebook)

Previously published in 2019 under the title *Take Back Your Time*

Printed in the United States of America

Scripture quotations are from THE HOLY BIBLE, NEW INTERNATIONAL
VERSION®, NIV® Copyright © 1973, 1978, 1984, 2011 by Biblica, Inc.®
Used by permission. All rights reserved worldwide.

The proprietor is represented by the Blythe Daniel Agency, Inc.

Baker Publishing Group publications use paper produced from sustainable
forestry practices and post-consumer waste whenever possible.

23   24   25   26   27   28   29        7   6   5   4   3   2   1

To my home team,

David, Ainsley, Connor, and Berkley,
time with you is the best time of all.

# Contents

# Acknowledgments

This book is a dream come true. I want to extend my deepest gratitude to the following:

My husband—David, for encouraging and supporting me, and most of all, for believing in me. I am beyond grateful that I get to do life with you.

My children—Ainsley, for being one of my best friends, always cheering me on, and gifting me my green tassel earrings; Connor, for your sweet compliments, timely advice, and serving as my go-to tech guy; and Berkley, for reminding me that life is meant to be full and fun and for sending me a life-giving text right when I needed it.

My parents—Steve and Janet, for your endless support and providing me with a firm foundation of faith, security, and love. You have both modeled to me how to prioritize and live life well.

My sisters—Haley, for all you do behind the scenes for MWM (I couldn't keep pace without you); and Harmony, for inspiring me with your entrepreneurial spirit.

My friends—Julie, Jenny, Jill, Cristina, and Jena, for allowing me to share your stories and touching my life with your incredible kindness.

My editor—Andrea Doering, for believing in me as a writer and giving me the opportunity to share my tips and tools.

My agent—Blythe Daniel, for your advice, support, and most of all, for seeing my potential.

She Speaks (Proverbs 31 Ministries), Hope Writers, and The Open Door Sisterhood, for helping me realize my dream of becoming an author.

# Introduction

The only reason for time is so that everything doesn't happen at once.

Albert Einstein

Are you blazing the corporate trail, feeling like you can't keep pace with the demands of both your career and your life? Are you attempting to balance home and work while also serving as an unpaid Uber driver for your children? Are you settling into a new season as an empty nester or a recent retiree, realizing you have more time than you ever dreamed of yet unsure how to best utilize this newfound freedom?

No matter your season, no matter your walk of life, no matter what time is requiring of you—this book is for you! If your desire is to *maximize time* and *minimize stress*, you are in the right place. Within the pages of this book, through stories and simple tools, you'll learn how to make successful time management your reality. It's time to take back your time!

*The Productivity Zone* was born from my own personal and profound experiences of living through five unique seasons. When I refer to seasons, I am referring not to the seasons of the calendar year but to the various and significant chapters of my life: from working full-time as a businesswoman, to being a stay-at-home mom (three kids in five years—hello stress!), to homeschooling my three elementary-age children, to living abroad, and most recently to working as an entrepreneur and navigating the ever-changing road of parenting teenagers.

In each of these seasons, I have experienced in a variety of ways the crushing reality of how complicated it can be to manage time well. Additionally, as a professional organizer, I observe firsthand the daily struggles my clients experience as they attempt to organize, plan, and schedule their time.

*Time management* can seem like a complicated concept, which it is and it isn't. Time management's nickname is *choices*. And how you choose to spend your time is a reflection of your priorities. Your choices are the fabric of your life. The way you carefully or haphazardly navigate your daily decisions will, intentionally or unintentionally, ultimately define your life. What you do within your seconds, minutes, hours, days, weeks, months, and years will determine your ability to accomplish your goals, realize your dreams, and live out your purpose. Bottom line, how you approach your choices is the deciding factor between your days being either peace-filled or panic-filled.

The good news? Although it may not be easy, it is simple to live simply. Living simply requires you to put book-ends around your commitments. It necessitates flexibility with the ebb and flow that life brings while also remaining steadfast and purposeful.

*The Productivity Zone* is filled with easy time-management tips to help guide you as you embrace your seasons of life. You'll learn how to implement three distinct time zones into your schedule and how to coordinate your life activities and tasks with these zones. I promise that these simple, translatable tools will help you to experience less hustle and more harmony.

And, trust me, I *know* hustle.

I've been "that mom." The mom who didn't know the name of her son's fourth-grade teacher—a month before the school year ended. The mom whose kitchen sink was usually stacked way too high with sticky and smelly dishes because everyone in my house always wants to eat. And unfortunately, I still have the tendency to think that I can cram eight hours of work, projects, or you name it into a four-hour time slot, which is the best way to induce an overwhelming sense of hurry.

Having experienced more hustle than I'd like to admit, I've learned that the mode of full throttle usually doesn't work. Sure, I find ways to get things done. I'll even show up on time or check off a box or two. But those hurried experiences tend to lack meaning, because I'm moving way too fast to enjoy or savor the moments. Activities become more of a blur than a blessing. Whereas, when I commit to remaining attentive to my specific purpose, in my current season, insisting that intentionality remain the heartbeat of my schedule, I'm able to realize more harmony and less hustle.

Time is always with you, walking alongside you on your journey and very much a part of your every experience. Whether in the mundane moments, the cherished memories, the obligatory daily duties, or the unwelcome trials—*your time is a responsibility, a privilege, and a gift*.

My hope and prayer is that you will find comfort, inspiration, and encouragement for how to organize your time well and live your most meaningful life.

Let's seek more harmony together, one day at a time.

# 1

# Your Time

## Steering Your Direction

Lack of direction, not lack of time, is the problem. We all have twenty-four-hour days.

Zig Ziglar

When we think about time management, we tend to think that the problem is we just don't have *enough* time. That is not the problem; it is a symptom of a different issue. The issue has much more to do with whether we are facing in the right direction as it relates to how we manage the time we have.

The day my husband came home and told me he wanted to put in for an overseas assignment for work, I was not thrilled—even though I'm the type of person who likes adventure and definitely prefers to go, see, and do. But his request to uproot our family of five to a foreign country for a minimum of three years seemed a bit, shall we say, disruptive. I suggested we might start by taking a couple's trip to Europe to, you know, sort of test the waters, as I had never even been outside of North America. My stalling suggestion didn't interest him in the least. Nor did my idea of considering a move to another state for his work.

"California has a nice climate. Maybe we could have a pool or a Tuscan-styled home?" Nope. He passionately desired a change, both personally and professionally, and ultimately, I was convicted to support my husband and faithfully trust in God's timing, planning, and direction.

So, yes, I said yes. A bit reluctantly, but I meant it, and it was a yes from me.

After almost a year, David was selected, and he was over the moon! I, on the other hand, was unsure, but I welcomed the news and set about working through all the logistics of preparing for an overseas move for a family of five and a cat. Talk about details, and I *love* details! I was optimistic that our new adventure would be an opportunity of a lifetime. I embraced our temporary (three-year) relocation with a positive attitude and even started to feel myself getting excited about our pending major life change.

Nine months later we shipped our car and boarded a plane in Portland, Oregon, on a dark, cold, January morning. We traveled for over twenty-four hours with twenty-plus oversized bags and our cat in tow to Lisbon, Portugal. The adventure began.

I remember our arrival and first few days and weeks like they were yesterday. We were shuttled to a hotel with an oceanfront view where we stayed for over two months. If you've never lived in a hotel for two months with three grade-school-age children (thankfully the cat was not with us for this stint), living out of suitcases while attending to regular life (like packing daily lunches for school), I don't recommend it. It was the longest and quite possibly the hardest two months of my life. Thankfully, our kids were absolute troopers and rolled through the transition with ease.

As soon as we had unpacked our suitcases, bought groceries, and purchased new phone plans, David began work in his new office and the kids jumped into their school year midway.

Then there was me—bound to our hotel with no car (which would take eight weeks to arrive) and living in a foreign country. The excitement wasn't sinking in—at all. I wish I could say that things got better for me. In some ways they did, but in many ways our three and a half years in Portugal felt somewhat like my time in a barren, dry desert, and yet we were five minutes from the beautiful ocean.

This season in my life rocked my world. It was the first time that almost every piece of my purpose or what fell under my umbrella of responsibility was stripped away from me. I still had a purpose in mothering and in my marriage, but beyond that, so much of my former life had disappeared. In Oregon, I had been teaching fitness classes, homeschooling the kids, volunteering, and managing (organizing, decorating, and running) our humble abode. My life was packed with purpose. My schedule was full, my time was allocated to my different priorities, and my direction was crystal clear.

When we settled into our new life in Portugal, I was sending my children off to school for a full eight hours a day and we were renting a home that didn't provide me the freedom to renovate and redesign (two of my passions). Instead, all I could do was creatively rearrange furniture and hang pictures to try to create some semblance of our style and make our rental house feel more like home. I desperately pursued finding part-time work—at the local health clubs, my husband's office, my children's school— but nothing fit or worked out for me. It was the first time in my life when one door after another kept slamming shut in my face, and I hit an all-time low. Furthermore, relocating over five thousand miles away from home revealed several cracks in our marriage that we had not previously seen. It seemed *maybe* part of God's plan was to strip away some of the fullness (some might call it busyness; more on this later) from my life to expose areas in our marriage that desperately needed attention and repair.

As I peeled back my layers of sadness, I realized that what was so incredibly hard for me in this season was that I lacked clear direction and purpose. I had all the time in the world, and yet I didn't have a productive way to use any of it. Sure, lunches and tennis lessons were fun, but I personally needed much, much more. I had not entered into our overseas season needing a break from the life I had already established.

In time, I was able to find my bearings on the map of my life and find my direction. I became intentional about setting goals for myself, and I began writing, blogging, and consulting as a personal trainer. More importantly, David and I worked very hard on our marriage, and our time in Portugal became the launching pad for a stronger and healthier relationship. We needed this extra time God had provided as a gift to invest in our relationship. We just had to open it.

## Embracing Your Season

The main takeaway from my season of life in Portugal, other than my newfound love for octopus and espresso, was that when it comes to time management, you must first embrace your current season. When you welcome your current season and marry it to your purposes, you are able to make deliberate choices surrounding your commitments. Knowing which direction to steer is vital to knowing your next steps.

Once I realized my purposes for my season in Portugal— working on my marriage, working as a personal trainer, serving through our church, and even running a marathon (one of my life goals)—I was more successful with my time management. Before identifying my specific purposes for this season, I was lacking direction, intention, and motivation. Because of this lack of purpose, I was unable to fully embrace it. But after defining my purposes for my season, things slowly fell into place and I no longer felt as if I had all of this time to fill and no way to fill it.

From this experience, I was reminded that each season provides new and different opportunities and that some seasons are more about being and waiting than doing and performing. I also learned a valuable lesson: having *too much* time can be just as challenging as having *too little* time.

With different seasons of life come different opportunities and obligations. Recognizing your current season of life is essential to knowing how to intentionally orchestrate your time. Embracing your season with a heavy dose of realism and optimism will equip you to be thoughtful and deliberate as you manage your time.

In chapter 2 you will work to discover your current three to five purposes. Your purposes can and will look different from season to season, and your number of purposes is whatever number is right for you. There really are no other rules.

Your current season may be one of growing, pruning, resting, or waiting. Whatever your season—claim it as yours. This is your time! Today is your day.

## Clearing Your Clutter

While we may think we don't have enough time, the one thing we all have enough of is—stuff!

Peter Walsh, the professional organizer from TLC's hit show *Clean Sweep*, shared the following:

> Every single person I met tells me not only about their own clutter problem, but the clutter problems of a family member, or those of a friend. Nobody seems immune. The stories are not dissimilar—papers and magazines run amok, garages overflow with unopened boxes, kids' toys fill rooms, and closets are so stuffed that it looks like the clothing department of a major retailer is having a fire sale. The epidemic of clutter, the seeming inability to get organized, and the sense that "the stuff" is taking over affects us all.[1]

Having too much stuff affects our time. Clutter is at the core of each and every one of our time-management challenges. Clutter is any single thing that is crowding and limiting us from moving forward positively in our life. It not only robs us of time but is also a distraction and a drain. *We are spending time managing our stuff rather than managing our time*.

Consider this. The average home in America has roughly three hundred thousand items in it—from plates, to pillows, to pictures.[2] The number of storage units is on the rise across the country, because consumers are continuing to buy, buy, buy and store, store, store. In fact, there are 88.6 square miles of self-storage facilities in America, almost three times the size of Manhattan, New York![3]

Why do we have so much clutter? One reason is because we are inundated with decisions almost every second of every day. There is such a thing as decision fatigue, and it often leads to paralysis by analysis. The upside of this challenge is that we have so many wonderful choices to choose from. The downside is that we are constantly bombarded with tiny decisions throughout the day. Too many choices result in the acquisition of too much clutter.

A second reason we have so much clutter is twofold: shopping is more convenient than ever, and items are more affordable than ever. It's easy to get a good deal almost anywhere we shop. I am completely guilty of this deal-hunting mentality, because I too like a good deal. Yes, Target one-dollar section, Costco bulk items, and Amazon one-click shopping—I'm talking about you!

These days, it's easy to accumulate more in less time. We can have something delivered to our doorstep in the blink of only two days—thank you, Amazon! We no longer have to trudge to the store to hunt for deals; the deals are coming to us. But are they *good* deals?

Here's the issue. Clutter is not just physical; there can also be mental and emotional clutter, and they are just as difficult to manage as physical clutter. I'm guessing you, like me, are probably weighed down by physical, mental, or emotional clutter—or maybe a combination of all three. One of the best things to do to rein in the burden of clutter and lighten our load is to clear as much of the clutter out of our life as possible.

Having excess clutter makes it hard to know where to start. How can we know what direction to steer if we don't even know where to begin?

To help make the most of your time, I want you to consider which forms of clutter are most negatively impacting your ability to manage your time. Honestly and gently assessing between the essentials and the nonessentials in your life will help you to create the room necessary for your priorities.

It's time to clear the clutter that is weighing you down. Use the questions in the next three sections to dig deeper into how clutter is affecting your time and your life season.

### Physical Clutter

I often find that our storage areas become our catchall spots, and I find myself feeling stressed whenever I have to walk through these areas or search for something. As you look around your home—possibly all three hundred thousand items (more or less)—look for patterns of clutter that are negatively impacting your time. Identify those things that are just taking up space, then answer the following questions:

▶ *When was the last time you actually used* _____ *(fill in the blank)?* If you have a hard time answering this question, you may have answered your decluttering question right off the bat! In general, don't keep things that you don't use at least once a year.

▶ *Where will you really use this "someday"?* Often you hold on to something because you think you'll need it someday. Ask yourself honestly if you will *really* use this item in the future. If the answer is no, don't keep it.

▶ *What is the cost of your time to keep this item?* Every single item you own requires something from you. Question if the value of keeping the item exceeds the cost of keeping it. Consider all the demands that your physical things (storage, maintenance, etc.) require of you.

### Mental Clutter

I regularly struggle with debilitating migraines, so I know all too well how mental clutter can increase stress. I intentionally work to minimize how much time I spend worrying and fretting about my life, whether it's mom guilt or work demands. It definitely takes effort not to worry, but the payoff—fewer migraines—is always worth it.

▶ *What do you tend to worry about?* If you are prone to worry and stress about life, this is naturally causing you internal chaos and adding to your mental clutter. You are likely focusing on things that are out of your control. Work to worry less and pour into those things that you *do* have some control over.

▶ *In what areas do you experience feelings of shame and guilt?* Be careful not to let these feelings crush and consume you. Press into them, identify them, and seek to forgive yourself (and others). Holding on to these feelings will increase your mental clutter and decrease your mental capacity.

▶ *When do you engage in negative self-talk?* What you tell yourself is often what you end up believing about yourself. Choosing to highlight your negative attributes rather than your positive ones is pointless. A critical spirit can keep you stuck. Determine to look at yourself through a positive lens, spotlighting your best traits.

### Emotional Clutter

Parenting teenagers has added to my emotional clutter! Not that I'm complaining. (Well, maybe a little.) One of the best ways I am able to manage the emotional clutter that comes from parenting three teenagers is to ensure that I keep my own emotional cup full. By finding ways to recharge and refill, I am able to meet the relational needs in my life and decrease the effects of emotional clutter.

▶ *What relationships are causing you more chaos than calm?* Seek relationships that are mutually life-giving and avoid letting obligation be the thing that keeps you connected, especially if it is an unhealthy relationship. Work to keep your emotional tank full so you can better navigate all your relationships.

▶ *What memories are you hanging on to out of sentiment rather than savoring the memory for what it was—a memory?* Memories are wonderful. They produce emotional (often happy and sometimes sad) feelings from your past. While memories and reflection are important, it is more important to live in the present. Holding on to items based on emotional ties can lead to accumulation of clutter, both emotional and physical.

▶ *What decisions are keeping you stuck and stagnant?* You have so much information at your fingertips that decision making can feel almost impossible. You can easily spend hours trying to make just one decision. To avoid getting cemented in indecision, consider your dreams and values. Stack every decision against these two things. Then keep it simple and don't overcomplicate your decision. It's often better to decide than to stay stagnant in indecision. Sometimes the best decision is to decide—and then make that decision right!

Less clutter equals more time—more time for the things you want to realize in your life. Refuse to let clutter remain an obstacle in your life. Clearing your clutter will create space for you to more fully embrace your season of life and to keep steering in the right direction. By removing the nonessentials from your life, you will naturally create more room for the essentials.

## Blending Quality and Quantity

No matter your season of life, I want to encourage you to adopt an attitude encompassing both quality and quantity, specifically when it comes to your time.

We've all heard the popular saying Quality over Quantity. Well, I'm going to agree to disagree. What we really want is quality *and* quantity. It's vital to find a balance between too much and too little, a balance in which the cost of your time is fully realized—where your time becomes a form of appreciation and your output reveals a high level of attention. If you focus on doing more, you will usually discover you are doing less.

Yes, you may be dropping off a casserole, serving in a classroom, coordinating a going-away party at work, or making time for a coffee chat. But if your heart isn't into your commitment, you won't experience the quality that should be found within the activity. However, if you intentionally put in the hours *and* invest your heart, you will reap more benefit and more likely find yourself in a win-win situation.

Time is exactly what you require to accomplish those things you need to do. When you combine quality and quantity, you will better reach your goals.

Quality refers to a high level of excellence. If something is worth doing, it should be worth doing well. A focus on quality will always help when scheduling your time. Seek a condition of quality in all of your life choices. If something is not bringing you value or is not adding quality to your life, choose to make a better choice! (Keep this in mind when you are shopping. Less is more.) Make it your mission to aim for quality. Saying a soft yes to life-giving choices and a strong no to life-draining choices will help you to increase the quality of your season of life. Remember, the word *no* can be a one-word sentence.

An example of a time in my life when I reaped the benefits of combining quality and quantity was when we had our first baby. David and I collectively and intentionally decided I would "retire" from working full-time and devote my time to raising our precious newborn. We agreed that I would continue to teach fitness classes a few times a week, but other than that, I would step down from working forty-five-plus hours a week outside of our home.

At the beginning of my pregnancy, we meticulously listed the financial priorities we wanted to accomplish before I left my job. The goals ranged from paying off our car, to buying a new appliance, to taking a holiday vacation before my February due date. We knew that without a calculated plan, it would be too tough of an adjustment financially for us to downsize to one full-time salary. Thankfully, our planning paid off (literally and figuratively), and my transition to being a stay-at-home mom went relatively smoothly. Other than the shock I experienced trying to figure out how to manage my time at home.

Before staying home, I was used to having the majority of my time managed for me via my work schedule. It required that I be at the office from eight to five, five days a week. It was a newfound freedom to stay home and not have a fixed schedule. Caring for a newborn was time intensive, but I found the bigger struggle was learning how to use and plan my time. It was a season that was all new to me.

Before we had Ainsley, we were nicely settled into the popular DINK (double income, no kids) way of life (the good ol' days!). That season consisted of going to movies every Sunday afternoon, because we could, and dinnertime parked in front of the TV. Our dinners usually consisted of some variety of grilled meat, a side of instant rice, and some overcooked vegetables—yum. Unless it was dog-obedience school night; then we routinely got Thai takeout. Please note, our dog, a Boxer named Princess Lea, won Most Improved in the class.

On the weekends, we grocery shopped and ran errands, got all the laundry done, and cleaned the house together. When time permitted, we tiled our bathroom and kitchen floors and painted every room in our house. We had a nice rhythm to our life, and we thought we had plenty of time despite our demanding jobs.

When I moved into my new season of being a stay-at-home mom, I hadn't anticipated how much more time we would collectively have. Our quality of life immediately improved. After making the transition, we soon recognized that our previous schedules hadn't allowed enough margin to enjoy our season. Balancing two careers, home management and maintenance, pets, and life in general had been a lot to handle. But when I became more available to grocery shop during the week, get the laundry done on a single day, and have dinner ready and waiting when David returned home at the end of the day, we were able to enjoy our time together so much more. Fewer to-do items were having to be squeezed into the evenings. Our weekends also became more relaxing and restorative. We didn't have a large home or a fancy car, nor did we go on lavish vacations, but we had a newfound and much-appreciated slower pace.

In this season, we discovered a new value we collectively shared. We both valued quality *and* quantity. We wanted to be available to one another and have increased time to experience more of our life together. We learned that—for us—less money meant more time. Less commitment meant more flexibility. Less busyness meant more fullness. Our choices resulted in our eyes opening to the value of quality and quantity. These values remain important to us to this day. We've remained intentional about having less stuff and more simplicity. We've made deliberate choices to align all commitments against the measure of quality and quantity.

I'm not saying that one parent should stay at home or that two working parents equal less quality or quantity of time. I share our experience simply to encourage you to look closely at the choices in your own life. Look at all your major decisions, from your location to your career, from your relationships to your responsibilities, and ask yourself if your choices are adding positivity or negativity to your life. Knowing how to determine the difference between the two will help you to better clarify your values and make intentional choices.

By choosing to be intentional with our life choices, both David and I have been able to achieve a better balance. We've both been able to pursue our individual purposes and have intentionally scheduled more margin into our calendars.

Just as quality matters when it comes to how you spend your time, quantity matters too! There will be times in your life seasons when the one thing you have to do is simply put in the time. But when you have a choice about how much you take on and the quantity of time required of you, the best way to approach your decision is to count the cost of that time.

When it comes to your calendar and how many items you add to your schedule, keep in mind that with every yes to something you are saying no to something else. If you overcrowd your schedule, you will soon find yourself sacrificing your level of output, and your productivity may actually decrease. With too much on your to-do list, you won't have the ability to focus. Too little time will be assigned to each detail and duty. Commit to knowing yourself and the amount of time necessary for you to complete the various priorities in your life season. The quantity of time you pour into your life choices will reap rewards.

*Quantity should remain best friends with quality for the best possible outcome.* The wonderful news is that you have enough time to do exactly what you are being called to do in your current season of life. Isn't that comforting?

In some seasons, like mine in Portugal, you may find you are spending much of your time waiting, like being stuck in a traffic jam. In other seasons, like mine as a new mother, you may find you are learning how to navigate new and unfamiliar terrain. Whatever your season, God has equipped you to be exactly where you are. He knows your destiny!

Taking back your time simply means knowing where to start. Andy Stanley says it best: "Direction—not intention—determines our destination."[4] In each and every season, seek to know your direction. Knowing where you want to go will help you to get there! Fully embrace your current season, clear the unnecessary clutter, and blend both quality and quantity. When you do, you will be able to minimize your stress and maximize your time.

### Tip—Ten Ways to Clear Clutter

- ▸ Use gift cards immediately and entirely.
- ▸ Don't take free product samples, brochures, menus, flyers, and so on.
- ▸ Delete apps, messages, texts, photos, and contacts you no longer need.
- ▸ Don't store music or movies you no longer listen to or watch.
- ▸ Clear the clutter from your car every time you get home.
- ▸ Don't keep expired foods, beauty products, and medicines.
- ▸ Shred or toss receipts as soon as possible.

- ▶ Don't hang on to outdated and unused clothing, electronics, and toys.
- ▶ Cancel services you no longer use or benefit from.
- ▶ Don't sign up for newsletters and emails that don't bring you value.

> Take back your time—
> steer your direction!

# 2

# Your Schedule

## Prioritizing Your Priorities

The key is not to prioritize what's on your schedule but to schedule your priorities.

Stephen Covey

As a professional organizer, I am hired by my clients to help them with the tasks of organizing and de-cluttering. I find that my clients, more often than not, are overwhelmed and cannot find the time in their schedule to work on these two critical tasks. They call me when they have reached a point at which they simply do not know where to begin nor what to do.

The common theme seems to be that most people are buried in their things or their commitments or a combination of both, and their life feels out of balance.

To get more organized, you have to first find, and then guard, adequate time in your schedule to work on organizing and decluttering. When I agree to work with a client, they are choosing to bring in coaching and account-ability. By deciding to work with me, they are blocking off a specific amount of time to work on calming their chaos. They are making organization a priority.

Decluttering and organizing a home or an office space are exhausting, slow-moving, and oftentimes emotional processes. However, over time my clients are able to shift from feeling overwhelmed to feeling empowered. And as a result, they have more time for their purposes and priorities.

While it is important to organize to maximize your time, it is just as vital to know what your purposes and priorities are. Without a clear understanding of your purposes in your current season, you will have a difficult time knowing how to prioritize your time.

Once you determine your purposes and priorities, you will have a better vision of what you are being called to do and the direction for how to schedule your time accordingly.

## Daily Five

With five people in my family, all moving in five different directions, my role is to keep things calm despite the chaos! One tried and tested time-saving tool we have used is what we call the Daily Five. The Daily Five lists the five tasks each of our children need to complete each day.

After getting tired of our daily morning dash that left no room for kind parting words or sweet goodbye kisses,

I sat down and thought through the common reminders we were giving our kids every day. After compiling a short list, I took the top five priorities and typed them up as a go-to for each of our children. Then I put a copy of the Daily Five on our fridge and placed a copy in their bedrooms as well. They are as follows:

1. Make bed, open shutters, tidy room and bath
2. Brush teeth (a.m. and p.m.)
3. Load *your* dishes (after every meal)
4. Put away backpack, shoes, lunch box, and coat
5. Complete daily chores by 4:00 p.m. (Monday–Thursday)

My thinking was that if I could refer my kids to the Daily Five in the form of a quick question, it would minimize the likelihood of hearing, "Oh, I didn't know I needed to do that." It would also help to put the responsibility for doing them on our kids rather than David and me having to constantly remind them.

Once our kids acknowledged they understood their daily duties, all we had to ask was "Have you done your Daily Five?" By clarifying their priorities on the front end, it helped them to better stay on task. It also created more time for kisses and hugs at the door, for snuggling up and reading on the couch, and best of all, for doing what kids do best—playing!

By implementing the Daily Five, we gave our kids a better starting point, and they rose to the occasion. We provided them with a better sense of direction and a clearer focus. As both students needing to get ready for school and family members needing to contribute to Team Tyree, they needed to do a better job of fulfilling their purposes. We taught them to prioritize their priorities!

## Purposes and Priorities

When I was midway through college, I learned a valuable lesson about purposes and priorities.

My parents told me at the beginning of my college career that they would help fund two-thirds of my in-state college costs for a maximum of four years. This sounded fantastic at the onset of my freshman year. And yes, this was extremely generous. However, when my junior year rolled around and I was put on academic probation (apparently earning below a 2.0 GPA is not advised—especially in back-to-back terms), I had a rude awakening. Basically, I wasn't on track to graduate on time, and I didn't have a way to pay for additional time in school.

A few not-so-nice letters from the school administration was just what I needed to help me realign my academic priorities (under the overarching purpose of working toward earning my college degree). I settled on a business administration degree and planned out my classes and credits for my senior year. After careful examination, I realized I needed to take a combined total of sixty-two credits over my last three terms of college to successfully graduate in four years. Generally, students take a maximum of eighteen credits per term, so I was going to have to go above and beyond the normal standards in order to graduate on time.

In my quest to better fulfill my academic priorities, I determined then and there that I would tackle the credit requirements head-on. I chose to be intentional about my college education; after all, this was one of my top purposes in this season of my life. I signed up for twenty credits for the fall term of my senior year. Not only did I take a full course load of no-coasting-allowed business classes, I also worked eight hours a week at an internship and taught several fitness classes every week. I am both happy and proud to say that I did it! I was able to graduate in four years, because I successfully completed the whopping total of sixty-two credits in three terms!

When I realized I was not on track to graduate on time, I knew I needed to realign what I was doing. My top three purposes for my senior year were school (finishing my degree), work (earning money), and relationships (faith, family, and friends). That was it. I had to spotlight my top three aims or purposes, shift gears, get to work, and then stay the course.

The lessons I learned that year about aligning my purposes and priorities will always remain with me. The experience taught me that different seasons of life demand different focuses and attention. Before my final year of college, I had been focusing my time on things that didn't fit my purposes or fall within my priorities. I was wasting time on wrong choices that did not align with my right priorities. Thankfully, because I made a series of intentional choices, I was able to make up for lost time, though this does not always happen.

When it comes to managing your time efficiently, you must begin by clearly identifying your purposes for the season you are in and then listing the individual priorities under each of your purposes.

I recently took some time to identify my main purposes in my current season of life, and I determined five overarching categories. I like to think of them together as a purpose umbrella, covering all I need to be doing. The purposes I clarified are general in nature but with subcategories that specify the priorities under each purpose.

Listing my current five purposes reminds me of what I should be committing to when I schedule my time. Without a clear plan for how I want to spend my time, I could easily spend it on things that don't fall under my purposes.

Your purposes are the top three to five areas in your life that you currently feel called to focus on and that God is prompting you to fulfill in your season. Think of these as your Daily Five or Weekly Five or Life Five—whatever helps you to best remember what they are. (Your number may be different, but you get the idea.)

Then, underneath your purposes, your priorities are what you are committed to doing in order to complete or accomplish each of your purposes. Listing your purposes and priorities will help you to better protect the time necessary for your essential tasks and to see and remove the nonessentials that don't belong on your calendar.

Again, to keep it simple and stay focused on your personal and professional time-management goals, whittle down your purposes to your top three to five. Being able to count them on one hand will help you to remember them. Seek the Lord's guidance as you consider where and to what you should be allocating your time. He has a purpose for you in your current season, and the more you press into his will for your life, the more peace you are sure to experience.

### *Morgan's Purposes and Priorities*

Here is a list of my purposes and priorities as an example.

**Purpose:** Home (management and maintenance)— managing our home in such a way that it is a sanctuary, a place of rest and relaxation, for our family.

**Priorities**

► Housework—maintaining a tidy home by following a weekly cleaning and laundry schedule.

► Food—planning weekly menus, shopping for groceries, and cooking meals in order to facilitate family time (and loud conversations) around the dinner table.

► Finances—paying bills, planning the budget, and aligning financial commitments with our financial goals.

**Purpose:** Work (organizing, teaching, and writing)— using my time, gifts, and talents to do the work God is calling me to do.

**Priorities**

► Client organizing sessions—working with clients to help them organize and declutter.

- ▶ Teaching and writing—teaching weekly fitness classes (sharing my passion for health and wellness) and writing (sharing my passion for organization and time management).
- ▶ Work (all other duties)—running my business and taking care of all administrative details (marketing, communication, billing, planning, advertising).

**Purpose:** Relationships—fostering authentic and healthy relationships with my family and friends.

**Priorities**

- ▶ Marriage and parenting—daily dedicating time to my relationships with my husband and children to demonstrate my love and commitment to them.
- ▶ Family and friends—connecting with those near and far to cultivate and sustain the closeness and community I desire.

**Purpose:** Volunteering—using my knowledge, skills, and abilities to serve my community.

**Priorities**

- ▶ Church and ministries—sharing encouragement and love by serving in MOPS, volunteering at church, and mentoring women.
- ▶ School and sports—supporting my children's school and sport activities when and where required.

**Purpose:** Personal—taking care of my health so that I may fulfill each one of my purposes.

## Priorities

- ▶ Spiritual—spending time in prayer, reading my Bible, and studying God's Word to equip myself with discernment and direction.

- ▶ Self-care—exercising regularly to decrease stress and increase stamina.

- ▶ Hobbies—investing in activities that energize me (reading a good book, taking a walk, playing tennis, sewing, etc.).

### *Your Purposes and Priorities*

Now it's your turn. List your purposes and priorities in the space provided.

**Purpose:** _____

**Priorities**

▶ _____

▶ _____

▶ _____

**Purpose:** _____

**Priorities**

▶ _____

▶ _____

▶ _____

**Purpose:** _____

**Priorities**

▶ _____

▶ _____

▶ _____

**Purpose:** _____

**Priorities**

▶ _____

▶ _____

▶ _____

**Purpose:** _____

**Priorities**

▶ _____

▶ _____

▶ _____

Now that you have determined your purposes and priorities, use this list as a gauge moving forward. Check the list when scheduling activities to make sure your commitments fall under one of your purposes. What you choose to commit your time to should always match up to one of your priorities.

If you are in a season in which you feel you have too little time, evaluate whether your choices are aligning with your purposes. In other words, what do you need to prune from your life to better grow into your purposes?

When you say yes to something, ask yourself if your yes falls under your purpose umbrella. Does your yes align with one of your purposes?

## Scheduling Snapshot

There has been more than a time or two when I've asked myself, *Where does my time go?* I feel as though time is slipping away from me. When I find myself feeling this way, I have learned to take a step back and examine where my time is really being spent.

One of the best ways to see where your time goes is to log your hours of activity over a seven-day period. When you look back over your schedule, you will see how and where your time was spent. After all, it *is* being spent!

By taking a snapshot of your calendar and tracking where you spend each hour for one week, you will discover how much time things really take and where your time is being spent hour by hour. You will also get a front-row seat to see what nonessentials you are spending time on.

Following is an example of a one-week schedule of mine.

By logging my hours for one week, I was able to see how much time I truly spent on different tasks. When I complete this exercise, I always gain new insights into how much time I am spending on the essentials and wasting on the nonessentials.

## Weekly Schedule: Time Log

| Time | Sunday | Monday | Tuesday | Wednesday | Thursday | Friday | Saturday |
|------|--------|--------|---------|-----------|----------|--------|----------|
| 6:00 a.m. | Get ready | Get ready/QT | Get ready/QT | Work: Write/Blog | Get ready/QT | Get ready/QT | Kids: Carpool |
| 7:00 a.m. | Work: Client | Home: Clean | Home: Clean/Prepare dinner | Work: Write/Blog | Home: Laundry | Home: Laundry | Home: Basement |
| 8:00 a.m. | Work: Client | Errands | Volunteer: MOPS | Home: Clean | Errands | Coffee with friend | Home: Basement |
| 9:00 a.m. | Work: Client | Work: Write | Volunteer: MOPS | Work: Client | Home: Laundry | Get ready | Home: Basement |
| 10:00 a.m. | Work: Client | Work: Write | Volunteer: MOPS | Work: Client | Family phone call | Home: House appt. | Home: Basement |
| 11:00 a.m. | Work: Client | Errands | Errands | Work: Client | Work: Client | Errands | Home: Basement |
| 12:00 p.m. | Work: Client | Work: Write | Home: Clean | Work: Client | Work: Client | Volunteer: Tea | Home: Basement |
| 1:00 p.m. | Work: Client | Home: Basement | Home: Basement | Work: Client | Volunteer: Tea | Volunteer: Tea | Home: Wrap Presents |
| 2:00 p.m. | Work: Client | Home: Basement | Home: Basement | Work: Client | Work: Client | Work: Emails | Volunteer: Family |
| 3:00 p.m. | Errands | Work: Write | Walk dog | Home: Clean | Kids: Ortho | Errands | Home: Basement |
| 4:00 p.m. | Errands | Walk dog | Kids: Swim meet | Kids | Kids: Carpool | Grocery shopping | Home: Basement |
| 5:00 p.m. | Home: Basement | Work: Emails | Kids: Swim meet | Home: Clean | Home: Cook dinner | Grocery shopping | Home: Finances |
| 6:00 p.m. | Home: Basement | Home: Cook dinner | Volunteer: Party | Date night | Christmas party | Home: Cook dinner | Home: Finances |
| 7:00 p.m. | Kids | Home: Clean | Volunteer: Party | Date night | Christmas party | Neighbor's party | Home: Dinner/takeout |
| 8:00 p.m. | Kids | Work: Write | Volunteer: Party | Home: TV | Christmas party | Neighbor's party | Home: TV |
| 9:00 p.m. | Home: Read | Home: TV | Volunteer: Party | Home: TV | Christmas party | Home: TV | Home: TV |

For example, before logging my hours, I thought I might be spending about eight hours a week sorting, washing, folding, and putting away laundry. After tracking my time, however, I discovered it's a total of three hours a week. Whereas when it comes to how much time I spend watching TV, I thought it might be around three hours a week but discovered it's actually six.

There is nothing right or wrong with the feedback from my time log. However, it's important to note whether you are appropriating your time to what you want to prioritize.

Yes, I want David and me to have clean clothes (my kids are responsible for doing their own laundry), and laundry falls under one of my purposes—home management and maintenance. So, three or even four hours per week spent doing laundry is more than fine by me! However, if I feel as though I do not have enough time available for exercise (one of my priorities), then I may want to consider limiting my hours spent watching TV and dedicate some of those to exercise.

You may be spending many hours on nonessential or nonpriority tasks, such as sitting in traffic, looking for lost items, or opening junk mail, just to name a few. Or it could be you have a hard time setting down your phone or getting off the computer.

This scheduling exercise is going to help you take back your time! You are going to evaluate how you actually spend your time—hour by hour and day by day. This tool and the information you glean from it will be vital as you continue to learn how to maximize your time!

After working through the week, you will have a better understanding of where your total weekly waking hours are being spent. You will see more clearly how your time is being allocated and where you might need to make some modifications to your schedule. By logging and tracking how you spend your time, you will be able to determine where adjustments within your schedule are needed to better accommodate your purposes and priorities.

You may also discover you have little windows of underutilized time you never realized before. Or you may find you are spending too much time on tasks that could easily be delegated to someone else. Or maybe, like me, you are surprised by how much time you spend cleaning your house (and asking why your house doesn't feel cleaner!).

It is easy to fall into the trap of mindlessly going through the motions. In life, it is easy to think you are spending more or less time on certain tasks than you really are. When you track where your time goes, you will have the facts; when you have the facts, you can adjust accordingly.

Using the following time log, go step-by-step through the exercise. (You may download a copy of the time log on my website, https://www.morganizewithme.com/shop.) It will take only seven days. While doing so, you may continue your reading by moving on to chapter 3 ("Your Productivity"). Be sure to continue completing the time log and to come back here to finish the remaining steps before jumping into chapter 4 ("Your Green Time Zone [GTZ]").

Are you ready to see how many hours you are spending where each week? Do you want to discover what

## Weekly Schedule: Time Log

| Time | Sunday | Monday | Tuesday | Wednesday | Thursday | Friday | Saturday |
|------|--------|--------|---------|-----------|----------|--------|----------|
|      |        |        |         |           |          |        |          |
|      |        |        |         |           |          |        |          |
|      |        |        |         |           |          |        |          |
|      |        |        |         |           |          |        |          |
|      |        |        |         |           |          |        |          |
|      |        |        |         |           |          |        |          |
|      |        |        |         |           |          |        |          |
|      |        |        |         |           |          |        |          |
|      |        |        |         |           |          |        |          |
|      |        |        |         |           |          |        |          |
|      |        |        |         |           |          |        |          |
|      |        |        |         |           |          |        |          |
|      |        |        |         |           |          |        |          |

nonessentials are filling up your schedule? Are you curious why you are often so tired at the end of the day?

Choose one week to list what you do each hour in the entire week. This can be any period of seven days in a row. List what you do as you do it. In other words, you are not proactively planning and plotting things on your schedule; you are reactively noting how you spend your time. The more detailed your log, the more it will impact your time management moving forward. Begin by filling in the waking hours you will be tracking. Remember, your schedule will be unique, just like you!

After taking a full week to complete your time log, now copy your purposes and priorities from your previous list to the summary below. Then look over your completed time log and list the time commitments you spent on each of your priorities. You may discover some priorities you are spending time on that you didn't list previously. If so, add these under the appropriate purpose and note the time spent on them. The more you differentiate the ways you spend your time, the more information you will have to work with as you approach managing your time in a new way. Keep in mind, this is only one week in your life, so remember to consider all extenuating factors (holiday, sickness, etc.) and document those factors accordingly. Parts of the week I tracked weren't typical of my weekly schedule. For example, I don't usually work on Sundays (we usually go to church), and I don't usually attend three parties in one week! This was a week in December, and there were more social gatherings than normal.

## Time Log—Summary

**Purpose:** _____

**Priorities**                                    Total Hours

▶ _____   _____

▶ _____   _____

▶ _____   _____

**Purpose:** _____

**Priorities**                                    Total Hours

▶ _____   _____

▶ _____   _____

▶ _____   _____

**Purpose:** _____

**Priorities**                                    Total Hours

▶ _____   _____

▶ _____   _____

▶ _____   _____

**Purpose:** _____

**Priorities**                          Total Hours

▶  _____   _____

▶  _____   _____

▶  _____   _____


**Purpose:** _____

**Priorities**                          Total Hours

▶  _____   _____

▶  _____   _____

▶  _____   _____

Now add up the total number of hours you spent on each of your purposes. I list mine below as an example. This is an interesting way to see how your time is divided between your top three to five purposes. There is not a correct percentage of how this should break down. What is important is that you determine if the numbers are within the ranges you would like to see for each of your purposes.

## Morgan's Hours per Purpose

**Purpose:** Home      Total hours:   42

**Purpose:** Work      Total hours:   27

**Purpose:** Relationships      Total hours:   18

**Purpose:** Volunteering      Total hours:   10

**Purpose:** Personal      Total hours:   15

## Your Hours per Purpose

**Purpose:** _____      Total hours: ____

**Purpose:** _____      Total hours: ____

**Purpose:** _____      Total hours: ____

**Purpose:** _____      Total hours: ____

**Purpose:** _____      Total hours: ____

Looking over your weekly schedule time log and the total number of hours per week that you spent on each of your purposes, answer the following questions:

► What essential activities and tasks did you spend your time on during the week? How did they align and match up with your priorities under each of your expressed purposes?

► What nonessential activities and tasks did you spend time on during the week? What commitments have you identified that need to be pruned from your schedule?

▶ What differences would you like to see in how you manage your time? Where do you need to make some adjustments in time allocations to your different priorities?

After taking this closer look at your current, real-life schedule, I hope you have an increased understanding and awareness of how you are spending your time and of the general categories that divide your time. Having a realistic view of how your time is being spent today will help you to invest your time more intentionally tomorrow. Time is a limited resource; take care of where and how you invest it!

After looking over the data from my time log, I found that I usually work somewhere between twenty-five and thirty-five hours a week, so it's no wonder that I often feel drained by the end of the week! It also revealed that I am spending upward of forty hours a week on the management and maintenance of our home (what?!). Both of these numbers were different from what I would have guessed. I thought they would be less. It's true that we were in the middle of a basement remodel when I tracked my hours, and this reality did affect the total number of hours I spent working on our home. However, all in all, the data I collected from a one-week snapshot reminds me why balancing work and home is challenging. It is also clear that both of these categories, home and work, require more time and commitment than I had realized.

If your time log stirred up things inside you and awakened a desire to do things differently, that's good news! Self-awareness is valuable. Like seeing yourself in a three-way mirror, it will help you to become an even better manager of your time. When you are the boss of your time, you are staying under your purpose umbrella despite the "weather" that life brings. When you stay under the protection of your umbrella, you will be more successful at getting done what you need to get done! *Whatever distractions rain down on you, you will be better prepared and more protected.*

The time log is a time-management tool that you can and should go back to time and time again. It is a great way to review how you are doing when it comes to your time management. Whenever you start to feel time slipping away or your health suffering or your stress levels skyrocketing, take a week and log your time to better understand how and why this is happening. This tool tracks your time after the fact and will always help to show you where some adjustments may be needed. It is an audit of your time, ultimately revealing your choices.

I also suggest that once you have finished reading *The Productivity Zone* and have implemented the easy time-management tools, you do another log of your time. It will be encouraging for you to see how your time-management skills have improved.

Commit to knowing your purposes for your current season. Write them down and keep them where you can see them daily ( just as I did with the Daily Five for our kids). Refer to your purposes every week and work to filter all commitments through your purposes, only prioritizing those things that are your true priorities.

Having determined and confirmed your direction and your priorities, it's time to grab your car keys and hop in the driver's seat! It's time to learn how to organize your day for optimal productivity.

### 🔆 Tip—Three Ways Timers Count

The next time you need to complete a task, try setting a timer. A timer is a helpful tool for either lengthening or limiting the time you dedicate to a specific task.

- ▶ To catch up on email, set a timer for twenty to thirty minutes. Then solely focus on reading and responding to emails. When the timer ends, stop and see what you have accomplished.

- ▶ To limit your time spent on social media, set a timer for ten to fifteen minutes. When the timer beeps, shut down the application or website and move on to your next to-do item.

- ▶ To organize or clean a space, set a timer for fifteen to thirty minutes and work only on that specific task. Turn off any and all distractions and get to work, stopping only when you hear the ding of the timer!

> Take back your time—
> schedule your priorities!

# 3

# Your Productivity

## Organizing Your Day

The way to get started is to quit talking and begin doing.

Walt Disney

**W**hen I examine those times I am extremely productive as opposed to the times I feel as though I get nothing done, I realize I gravitate toward two diametrically opposed types of days.

There is Day Number One. I'm behaving and working like an ambitious ant. I'm dotting my i's and crossing my t's. I'm feeling motivated and driven. I have an attitude that says, "Nothing is going to hold me back!" I feel purposeful, ready to take on the day, and determined to take care of my numerous daily tasks, both personal and professional. I have dinner in the Crock-Pot by 8:00 a.m. sharp, and I'm wearing my yoga pants because I'm actually planning to go to yoga versus my other kind of yoga—which looks more like grocery shopping. I'm patient *and* present with my children, the kitchen sink is miraculously empty and clean, my to-do list feels manageable, and sometimes I can still see faint vacuum lines in the carpet. It's an A-plus kind of a day!

*Day Number One feels like the definition of calm, cool, and collected.*

Then there is Day Number Two. I'm operating more like a floundering fish. I lack focus, my sense of purpose feels off, and I feel severely directionally challenged. I'm trying to put out the fires that are starting faster than I can handle—as if I am starting fires with one hand and rushing to put them out with the other hand. I usually realize midday that I have absolutely no conceivable plan for dinner (other than takeout). I keep washing the same load of clothes because I can't seem to stay on top of switching the load to the dryer before it gets gross and stinky. Showering feels like *way* too much effort, which leads to a frantic search for my dry shampoo. (When I eventually find it, the bottle is in my daughter's room—completely empty.) Being able to finish anything seems impossible, and of course, someone in my family has either thrown up, lost something, overslept, or is immersed in some end-of-the-world crisis. On this type of day, I want a do-over and an opportunity to press the "easy" button. Nothing feels easy on my Day Number Two!

*Day Number Two feels like the definition of chaotic, crazy, and catastrophic.*

The comforting part? I've learned that both versions of my days are OK. Inevitably, some days will go exactly as

I've planned and other days will go exactly the opposite of how I've planned. There will be days when I have an abundance of motivation and focus, and there will be days when I flat-out struggle to begin and don't have the time or energy to finish anything.

It's important to acknowledge that these two different versions of my day can and will be realities for all of us from time to time. Sometimes a Day Number One can turn into a Day Number Two and vice versa. If you accept the fact that the productivity of your days will always be subject to a variety of factors—your mood, energy level, mental capacity, and surroundings (people and environment)—you will be much more adaptable to whatever comes your way. And if you respond to a situation with a calm approach (even if thick in the throes of a Day Number Two), you can minimize your stress, maintain more peace with the people in your life, and not waste as much of your time and energy overreacting.

When you begin with a vision of intentionally organizing your day, you will become more of an actor rather than a reactor. You will learn to plan, plan, plan, and then go with the flow. Life is always moving, and it can oftentimes be very, very messy. A friend recently referred to her life as a "beautiful mess." I love that attitude! In this chapter you are going to learn how to embrace the mess while also carefully balancing the need to be productive.

In the next section, you'll learn about the three key attitudes that will help you to plan, organize, and construct your day, resulting in improved levels of productivity and output. Or in simpler terms, less panic and more peace.

## Mission, Motto, Mindset

First things first! I want you to completely delete the word *busy* from your vocabulary. Guy Kawasaki says, "Let's stop the glorification of busy."[1] I love this!

Let's look at some of the synonyms for *busy*: unavailable, buried, hustling, overloaded, swamped, occupied. These are *not* the kind of words I want to use when describing how I feel or how I'm spending my time. I want to be able to say that my life is *full*—full of value, purpose, and meaning. This is my mission. I desire to pursue all kinds of different endeavors and to be stretched in how I use my time, energy, and resources, but never at the cost of feeling overloaded, buried, or unavailable. I want a clear balance of quantity plus quality!

In his book *Procrastinate on Purpose: 5 Permissions to Multiply Your Time*, Rory Vaden writes:

> Quit telling everyone how busy you are. Resist the indulgence of saying "I am too busy."
>
> Your problem is not that you are too busy; your problem is that you don't own your situation.
>
> You get stressed and frustrated with distractions, fine—we all do. But your life is your responsibility. Any commitments you have were either made or allowed by you.
>
> It's not even right to complain or whine to others about how busy you are. You and I have the same amount of time in a day as Gandhi, Dr. Martin Luther King Jr., Mother Teresa, Michael Jordan, or anyone else who has achieved greatness.
>
> Once you own your problem, you empower yourself to create your own solution.

So, the first step is to get over our self-indulgent com-plaining about how we're so busy or there just isn't enough time in a day. If you are saying those things to yourself, then you are allowing yourself to be a victim—like I was.

You are not a victim. You are in charge. You are ca-pable. You are powerful enough to decide what you will and won't do with your time.

But one thing you are not is too busy.[2]

Haven't we all been in this predicament—when we *feel* busy? When we are maxed out, stressed to the limit, and too exhausted to fully enjoy our day-to-day lives?

The emotions related to feeling maxed out are often re-alities, even though we have more modern-day time-saving conveniences than ever before. Or do we? I think what we really have are more distractions, activities, choices, and wonderful ways of wasting our time than ever before. Hello, binge-watching *Friday Night Lights*!

We also have other people's demands on our time. People need us and they need our time. These create a feeling of a time crunch. With the many decisions to make surrounding the use of our time, it is imperative to keep intentionality as the foundation of our decision-making process. As Vaden says, "You are not a victim. You are in charge. You are capable. You are powerful enough to decide what you will and won't do with your time."

You have the power to choose a life of fullness and to set aside the draining existence of being overwhelmed and busy, but you will need to make that deliberate and intentional choice. Choose to remove *busy* from your vocabulary and prepare to welcome a fuller life—a life full of purpose, meaning, and value. No more frantic, only full.

I like to think of fullness this way: when I go to a coffee shop and purchase a chai tea latte, I expect to receive a full cup of tea. I desire a full serving. What I don't want is an overflowing cup of tea. If my tea spills over and makes a mess or burns my hands, then my positive experience is immediately altered. Likewise, I would be frustrated if served only a half cup of tea. I want to enjoy a full cup of my favorite beverage. A full cup of tea is what I expect and invested in.

We are created to desire fullness, and so we make that our mission. We are designed to use our time and talents to bless others. When we live a life of fullness, we will better fulfill our purposes.

In regard to your choices and commitments, seek a sense of harmony in how you schedule your time. Look for the sweet spot somewhere in the middle—somewhere between scheduling too little and scheduling too much. I feel a sense of peace when I have enough to do but not too much to do. Time is limited, as are your capacities. Aim to experience the Goldilocks-style "just right" feeling with your time. She picked just the right temperature of food, size of chair, and softness of bed—you know the story.

In keeping with our family mission of being focused on fullness, a while back we examined two obligations we had made. When evaluating our schedule and the stress around it, we collectively identified two commitments that were negatively impacting our family's schedule. They were creating stress and contributing to more busyness than blessing.

The first choice we had to make in seeking fullness was regarding my job at a health club. When we moved back to the States from Portugal, I was very excited to resume teaching fitness classes. However, as my new job and teaching commitment got underway, I saw the negative impact it was having on my family and me. I wasn't home two afternoons during the week, which happened to be the same time of day my kids were arriving home from school. On those days, dinners were often an afterthought (unless I was experiencing a Day Number One), and my mental energies were overly focused on memorizing choreography. Besides that, the job required that I recertify and invest in several weekend training sessions. My email inbox was constantly inundated with emails from my employer requiring either a response or some sort of a to-do on my part. This job, during this season of my life, cost too much. The conditions were less than ideal, and the job was contributing to an overwhelming amount of mental and emotional clutter.

After a few months and many long discussions, David and I agreed that instructing classes at this club was no longer a win for me and had become a drain on our entire family. We agreed that there must be a better solution out there.

When I took a step back, I was reminded that things can often look better on paper than when you get to the actual production or output phase of the commitment. The decision to take a break from teaching classes benefited all of us collectively. I'm happy to report that within a few months, I was hired at a different health club that was a much better fit for me and the entire family.

The second choice we made with regard to fullness was removing our daughter from her year-round competitive swim team. She enjoys swimming and loved being involved with her high school swim team, so we thought there was value in having her continue her swim training year-round. However, the commitment had become a serious time thief not only for her but also for all of us.

Before we made the decision to take her off the team, she and I had many conversations about why it wasn't working. She commented that her two-hour-long practices several nights a week (sometimes as many as five nights), coupled with a total commute time of close to forty-five minutes, were demanding too much of her time. Time that she could be using to work on her homework or recoup from her long days at school. They were also keeping me out in the evenings, which affected the rest of the family. We brainstormed other options and came up with a better choice. We added her to our health-club membership (for a fraction of the cost we were paying to the swim team), which allowed her to swim when it worked for her—and the rest of us too! We saved money and, most importantly, time.

As a family, we honestly reflected on and discussed these two decisions, and in doing so we agreed to say no to two good things. This required that we carefully consider the bigger picture. As Rory Vaden says, "Any commitments you have were either made or allowed by you." In other words, you can choose not to become buried by your schedule, but it will require reflection and self-awareness.

In *The Best Yes*, Lysa TerKeurst writes, "Every day we make choices. Then our choices make us. We have options. We make choices. Then we live the lingering effects, good and bad, of those decisions. And those decisions determine so much about our lives."[3] Commit to examining every commitment. Be discerning when an invitation, request, opportunity, or activity comes your way. Your goal is to fill up your cup with only those commitments that provide you with the most meaning. Opt exclusively for those choices that closely align with your values and purposes. Then organize your day with a laser-like focus solely on *fullness* rather than busyness. Fullness will look like contentment, purpose, and memories. A full life is a good life.

Every mission needs a motto, and this is ours: margin. I'll never forget those times when I didn't allow enough margin in my schedule, and I was left feeling underprepared, embarrassed, and frustrated. One experience, unfortunately, is burned into my memory. I had asked my friend Julie if she could watch my almost-one-year-old daughter while I went to the eye doctor. She agreed to help me, but I had scheduled it too close to an earlier commitment. On the day of the appointment, due to my self-induced, supertight schedule, I found myself hurrying home, screeching into the driveway, and rushing to pack some sort of lunch to take to Julie's house for Ainsley.

With only about two minutes to spare (I'm being generous), I quickly and without thinking (obviously) grabbed my husband's leftover tuna-fish-and-cottage-cheese mixture that was already conveniently packaged in a to-go container.

Yes, you read that correctly. It was a leftover mixture of tuna fish *and* cottage cheese. Not a nice helping of leftover lasagna, a baby-sized cup of vegetable soup, or a serving of my homemade mac and cheese. You know, basically anything that a baby would want to eat! (In my defense, my health nut of a husband had told me that he had fed this to Ainsley and she liked it.) I raced over to Julie's house, dropped off my baby girl, and told her that I had packed a lunch for Ainsley, even mentioning what it was. I felt it necessary to share that David had fed this concoction to her before. I clearly was trying to cover up for the fact that I hadn't planned very well at all.

After about an hour, I made my way back to Julie's to pick up Ainsley, and Julie and I spent some time catching up. She mentioned (very graciously) that Ainsley didn't really care for the tuna-and-cottage-cheese combo (what a surprise) that I had so frantically packed. Julie opted instead to feed her a serving of her leftover casserole, which Ainsley gobbled up. I laughed the whole thing off and thanked Julie for watching Ainsley and for sharing her food. But I left her house feeling not only embarrassed but also at capacity and very much like I had dropped the ball.

On the drive home I thought, *Why had I stacked my commitments so close together? Why didn't I plan better?*

*Why had I not taken the time to prepack an appropriate lunch for my baby?*

My daughter having a less-than-desirable lunch option was not the end of the world, of course. However, I learned a valuable lesson that day: it is critical to build adequate margins around our commitments. By creating a buffer, we make room for the smaller details and duties in our lives. More margin enables and helps us to respond and react to what comes our way.

Plan your commitments with generous margin. Adequate space within your scheduling should be your motto. When you allow your schedule to include the margin it demands, you'll be able to relax more and stress less. And most of all, you will be prepared and on time!

Along with having healthy margins, you will also want to have a mindset that can adapt to the changes that come your way. Adaptability, in regard to your schedule, is essential!

Over the years, I've identified that it's neither necessary nor required for me to be *overly* focused on the future. Even though I love pulling out my calendar and looking ahead at upcoming events and activities, I've learned that there is usually not much added benefit in planning too far out or stressing about potential time-management conflicts. I've discovered that when I become too concerned with the potential what-ifs of the future, I end up wasting my time and energy in the here and now.

On countless occasions, I have worried about potential scheduling conflicts, such as making sure I have adequate childcare coverage or thinking I need to reschedule an appointment because of a double booking. More often than not, however, the potential conflicts seem to work themselves out. My child gets invited to a playdate and I no longer need to arrange for childcare. A sports practice gets canceled due to bad weather and I'm able to make my appointment after all—double-booking problem averted!

By no means am I saying that you should not strive to be a proactive planner. What I am suggesting is that you take a deep breath and make a point not to overly stress about the potential and looming what-ifs!

Schedule changes will inevitably pop up, and plans may evolve. Things will happen that you weren't expecting and certainly weren't planning for. The best way to manage the unknown is to be better prepared with your reaction. Being flexible and adaptable will help you to respond as a *victor*, not a *victim*, of your circumstances.

To be victorious, an adaptable mindset is required. It will help you to successfully bend and flex as you battle against the demands of your schedule.

## Understanding Your Productivity

All times of the day are not created equal. Knowing the times within your day when you are most productive and least productive will help you to better schedule certain activities. You tick a certain way in rhythm with your own unique internal clock. The more you understand your natural rhythms, the more intentional you can be when organizing your day. Scheduling time to work on focused and intensive items during your most productive times of the day will naturally increase your ability to finish what you start.

When during the day do you feel the most productive and the least productive? Look for the patterns and trends in your answers to the following questions:

- In your current season, are you more of a night owl or an early bird?
- Which times of the day can you more easily multi-task: early morning, midmorning, early afternoon, midafternoon, early evening, midevening, or late at night?
- Do you like to work for longer periods with longer breaks or shorter periods with shorter breaks?
- When do you generally focus the best—morning, afternoon, or evening?
- When do you like to unwind and relax? Are there multiple times throughout the day that you like to slow down and take time to recharge?

My first job after college was working for a large department store as one of their store managers. It was a demanding job but one from which I learned so much. I worked with a team of six other managers, and we had a rotating schedule. It was essential that a store manager always be scheduled and available. We were the ones responsible for opening and closing the store, locking and setting the building alarm, and verifying all bank deposits. Due to the nature of retail, we had to be flexible and willing to work various shifts. It was not uncommon for me to open the store at 3:00 a.m. and two days later close down the store at midnight.

I was young and vibrant, and working an average of fifty-plus hours a week was fine by me. I enjoyed the pace and almost seemed to thrive on it. However, after some time on the job, my body started to react negatively to the scheduling changes. I was rarely eating at the same time of the day, my bedtime was constantly in flux, and I rotated between getting large chunks of time to sleep and what felt like short naps between shifts. Overall, I was exhausted and my digestive system was out of whack. This eventually led me to the doctor, who diagnosed me with some syndrome I knew I didn't have.

I continued to muddle my way through, and when I eventually left that job, my symptoms immediately went away. It was evident that my lack of a consistent schedule had negatively affected my health and well-being. The external requirements of my schedule were adversely impacting my internal rhythms.

I learned the hard way that protecting your daily schedule and having a consistent rhythm is good not only for productivity but also for protecting your health. Finding a happy melody between your internal rhythms and external rhythms is always worth the intentional effort.

The more you can identify and adjust how you naturally operate, the more accomplished you'll be. Working with your internal clock will increase your production level and decrease your stress level. You can, and should, choose your own style of music and then dance to it with intention, always considering your mental, emotional, and physical health.

You may be able to handle a schedule like I had at the department store; it might not be a problem for you. Or you may be like me and prefer a more consistent routine. I like flexibility in my day-to-day schedule, but I also know I do better in life when I go to sleep and wake up at the same time each day. Because this is important for me, I use it as a benchmark when evaluating my commitments. Understand too that where you are in your current season may drastically differ from previous seasons of life. Life is fluid, and as in nature, seasons change. Therefore, your internal rhythms may need adjusting.

For example, when my kids were younger, I was the true definition of a night owl. This was because as early as 7:00 p.m., all three of them were snuggled in their beds (I miss those days!), which meant that by 7:05 p.m., David and I could be settled on our comfy sofa, watching a TV show and enjoying bowls of ice cream and brownies. David would often retreat to bed earlier than me (he's always been more of an early bird), and I would generally begin working on something. Whether scrapbooking, paying bills, sewing, or reading, I craved these extended evening hours. They were my protected, calm, and quiet hours. This time in my day was rarely interrupted. I could almost guarantee that I would be able to get some things done, and it energized me. This was my routine for over a decade—and then things shifted.

My toddlers became teenagers, and no matter how hard we try, they just don't like to go to bed at 7:00 p.m.! Also, both of my daughters started having early morning swim practices, which meant I needed to get up before 5:00 a.m. to shuttle them to and from practice. Oh joy!

During this new season, I completely transitioned from a dedicated night owl to a reluctant early bird. The shift also meant that David and I were going to bed earlier and earlier—sometimes even before our kids! I discovered in this new season that I had an increased amount of energy and focus in the early morning hours because I had completely shifted my schedule and routine. It's interesting to me how my internal rhythms transitioned with my seasonal change of life. These days, I'm much more of a morning person, and I don't save any of my important tasks for the evening hours. My new peaks (productive times) are my morning hours, and my valleys (nonproductive times) are my evening hours.

In your current season, analyze and reflect on your internal clock and use it to self-rate a twelve-to-sixteen-hour chart. Completing the productivity chart will help you to determine your most and least productive times throughout the day, which will help you to organize your life with an increased level of intentionality.

Don't forget: your mission is fullness; your motto is margin; your mindset is adaptability! These three attitudes are the keys to making the chart work for you. Be generous with the amount of downtime you need. Be honest about how long you are able to concentrate. Be realistic about the amount of sleep you need each night. Be self-aware and seek feedback to help fine-tune your chart. *Ready, set, go!*

## Productivity Chart

Fill in the times that align with the hours you are awake each day. Then self-rate your peaks (productive times) and valleys (nonproductive times). Circle one star ( ★ ) for your lowest-productivity times, two stars ( ★ ★ ) for your medium-productivity times, and three stars ( ★ ★ ★ ) for your highest-productivity times.

| **A.M. Hours** | **Productivity Star Rating** |
|---|---|
| _____:00 | ★ ★ ★ |
| _____:00 | ★ ★ ★ |
| _____:00 | ★ ★ ★ |
| _____:00 | ★ ★ ★ |
| _____:00 | ★ ★ ★ |
| _____:00 | ★ ★ ★ |
| _____:00 | ★ ★ ★ |
| _____:00 | ★ ★ ★ |
| _____:00 | ★ ★ ★ |
| _____:00 | ★ ★ ★ |
| _____:00 | ★ ★ ★ |
| _____:00 | ★ ★ ★ |

| P.M. Hours | Productivity Star Rating |
|------------|--------------------------|
| _____:00 | ★ ★ ★ |
| _____:00 | ★ ★ ★ |
| _____:00 | ★ ★ ★ |
| _____:00 | ★ ★ ★ |
| _____:00 | ★ ★ ★ |
| _____:00 | ★ ★ ★ |
| _____:00 | ★ ★ ★ |
| _____:00 | ★ ★ ★ |
| _____:00 | ★ ★ ★ |
| _____:00 | ★ ★ ★ |
| _____:00 | ★ ★ ★ |
| _____:00 | ★ ★ ★ |

Later, you will use your productivity chart again to work on the important task of organizing your time into three different and specific time zones. Identifying your natural rhythms will help you to protect your much-needed time for self-care, allow you to accomplish more in less time, and assist you during those times when you must multitask. Your star rankings will help you assess which time zones coordinate with your tasks and responsibilities. Ultimately, my goal for you with the productivity chart is that you will be better able to maintain a sense of peace and harmony as you go about your day.

If I had been attempting to scrapbook when my toddlers were up, running around and getting into everything, I would have made snail-speed progress. By saving this time-intensive task for the late-night hours, I was matching my energies with my efforts. These days, I'm getting up before my kids just so I can finish a great book.

For now, my rhythm has shifted to that of an early bird. I've heard there is a worm in the deal, but who wants a worm? I would just as soon opt for the tuna and cottage cheese!

## Tip—Three Ways to Take Back Your Time

▶ Take more breaks (keep your tank full).

▶ Take on less (accomplish what matters most).

▶ Take small steps (work one step at a time).

> Take back your time—
> seek fullness, schedule margin,
> and stay adaptable!

# 4

# Your Green Time Zone (GTZ)

## Focus Time

> One of the saddest mistakes in time management is the propensity of people to spend the two most productive hours of their day on things that don't require high cognitive capacity (like social media). If we could salvage those precious hours, most of us would be much more successful in accomplishing what we truly want.
>
> Dan Ariely

ow we'll dive into what I call my *no-frills approach* to time management. Whatever your current season of life, you'll be able to use this easy-to-follow system starting today. With this approach, you will accomplish more of what you need to get done.

I like functionality and practicality, which is exactly what the time zones represent. Using the three zones provides a simple way to organize your priorities and schedule your time.

The first zone is the Green Time Zone (GTZ). In this zone, your primary goal is to *check the box*. You are committed to finishing one task at a time. From your productivity chart (chap. 3), you will use the hours in your day at which you circled three stars. This is when you'll work on the items that fall within your top and most important priorities, those that require a high level of attention, such as preparing a presentation, balancing a spreadsheet—or teaching a teenager how to drive.

I had never given this teenage rite of passage, or what I am now calling a serious *challenge*, much thought. Instructing a new driver how to drive is like teaching someone how to knit a sweater with your hands tied behind your back! The whole process felt surprisingly overwhelming and extremely scary to me, and it might just be the perfect definition of *out of control*.

A few months into the endeavor, and after some not-so-pleasant driving sessions, I realized my daughter and I needed to find a way to overcome these instructional obstacles and create a way to work better together. Especially if we wanted to meet our collective goal of developing a successful teen driver. I needed to establish some basic guidelines for our instructional driving time.

I told Ainsley that before our driving lessons, I had to be well rested, not be hungry in the slightest, and have enough emotional and mental energy to be in full-blown driving-teacher mode. Basically, I needed to have a lot of moxie or vigor to handle the twists and turns required for being her teacher (no pun intended). Likewise, I asked Ainsley to be in a good space, a time when she was not stressed about homework, had enough rest, and wasn't dying for a snack. We did not need any hangry attitudes in the driver's seat *or* in the passenger's seat.

For our driving lessons to be fruitful, both teacher and student needed some pep in our step. Just *hoping* that our driving time together would be productive was not going to cut it. We needed to deliberately plan for success. The beauty is that when we both mutually respected and followed the established and agreed-upon guidelines, we collectively experienced more progress and lowered the potential for problems.

The way we approached our driving time is the same manner in which you will want to set up your GTZ. In your GTZ, you will be addressing those items that fall within your top priorities. You will want to utilize a laser-like focus in this time zone because these are the hours in which you will be working on your most detailed or difficult tasks.

In the GTZ, you will commit to working on and finishing only one task at a time. Your goal will be to check off items on your to-do list deliberately and intentionally. You will clearly aim for a precise target. By identifying and establishing this time zone, you will experience more success with your output. An easy and memorable way to remember your GTZ and the attitude to take is to think of it as your time to focus.

## Moxie

In your GTZ, you will move things from start to finish and complete time-sensitive, top-priority tasks. To stay focused in your GTZ hours, you need to use moxie.

*Moxie* means vigor, verve, courage, pep, and know-how.[1] It could also be thought of as *gusto*. I first heard the word *moxie* in the movie *Lost in Yonkers*, which was set during World War II. The movie tells the story of two brothers who are sent to live with their domineering grandmother after their mother's death. There is a scene in which the dad (played by Richard Dreyfuss) is commending his eldest son on having moxie, to which his son asks, "What's moxie?"

Dreyfuss turns to his younger son and tells him to explain moxie to his brother. The younger brother responds by taking a solid stance of determination, like a fighter, and mimics pushing up his sleeves one at a time with a demeanor that says, "YOU want to mess with me?" With his hands he motions, "Come on," like a tough guy who says, "Bring it on, I'm ready to fight!"

I like the word *moxie* because to me it sums up the attitude and mentality you should possess when you commit to working on the tasks, priorities, and to-dos during your GTZ. A woman who says, "Yes, I can do this, even if I have to fight the distractions to do it!" has moxie. Taking your time, choosing to courageously embrace your abilities, and remaining focused with every single decision you make requires moxie.

Think of it this way. Moxie says, "I'm going to do what I have to do to get it done!" whatever "it" is. When you are working in your GTZ, you are using moxie and being decisive. You are pushing up your sleeves, or wearing 3/4 sleeves (whichever you prefer), and deliberately staying the course. You are choosing to focus your attention, remain intentional, and work on precisely what you have decided to work on despite potential roadblocks or distractions.

My lovely friend Jenny has been an inspiring example for me of what a moxie attitude looks like and how to authentically use moxie to navigate through life. I met Jenny via an email in which she informed me that she and her husband were going to be our sponsors for our upcoming overseas move. Thankfully, David's employer had assigned a family to show us the ropes. I didn't even know we were to be sponsored, so I was super excited! This was someone assigned to me, whom I could pepper with questions—a real relief to my organizing, planning, and detail-obsessing self.

Jenny began as a pen pal and turned into much, much more. I bombarded her with a million questions, important things: "Do you have a good hair person you can recommend? Do I need to learn Portuguese? What about rabbit; do I have to eat it? What is it like living there? Is driving in Portugal super crazy? Will I be able to buy the makeup I use in Portugal? Do I need to learn how to surf? Can I find cute clothes? How are the schools? Can I bring my minivan?" On and on, I tell you.

Jenny was a veteran in overseas living. I think she survived (I do not use this term lightly) ten consecutive years in several different countries. She provided me with a sense of understanding that yes, living abroad *is* hard. However, she also modeled a determined spirit. She made my transition to overseas living much easier and smoother. Not just because she gave me the much-needed information I desired, but also because she demonstrated the how-to. She showed me how to embrace my new season with a moxie attitude. She modeled how to dig in, push up my sleeves, and take on the challenges. Jenny encouraged me to get up and make a life for myself in Portugal—to push through the hard, use my time intentionally, and ultimately remain purposeful. She is the perfect example of how to approach working in your GTZ with a moxie attitude!

Again, your GTZ hours are going to center on the attitude of simply doing one thing at a time. Often the reality is that we tend to begin several projects (to-do items) all at once instead of starting and finishing one project at a time. There are times when our projects will and should stay open. Many tasks do require extended time and space to process or complete. However, when you determine to start and finish projects one at a time, you will experience the wonderful sensation of a job well done and in a timely fashion.

This can be as simple as dedicating one solid hour to organizing and responding to all your emails—check. Yes, you'll quickly receive more emails. However, if you focus on checking the box of working on your email correspondence for one hour, you'll be able to experience a sense of accomplishment. There will naturally be less chaos when you determine to intentionally complete your tasks with an individualistic and focused approach. Checking the box translates to doing only one thing at a time and to doing that one thing well.

During my GTZ hours, I work on my most detailed jobs, such as budgeting, invoicing clients, writing time-intensive emails, or making important phone calls. By intentionally saving these tasks for my protected GTZ hours, I am better able to make the necessary progress required for them. My scheduled hours vary from day to day and week to week, depending on my obligations and timelines. What doesn't vary is my level of focus in this time zone.

I want you to adopt the same moxie attitude that Jenny revealed to me. Working in your GTZ requires and demands that you take a determined stance, like a fighter, and guard your time for your priorities. Imagine putting on a pair of (cute, hot pink) boxing gloves when you begin working in your GTZ and saying, "Hey, people [whoever your people are], I've got work *to do!*"

Then keep it simple, focus, and *do* the work.

## Business Lady

In middle school, I was affectionately given the nickname Business Lady. This was not because I was all business when it came to my schoolwork. I think it had more to do with my early-onset, borderline-obsessive organizational skills and because I consistently demonstrated follow-through, especially with the things that were important to me.

I secretly loved the nickname and would spend time daydreaming about my future. I imagined my future self—dressed in professional business suits, preparing critical year-end reports, and rushing to and from important business meetings. I mean, after all, a Business Lady is a person who means business. (These days, you should see me tackle my to-do list when I am in my Business Lady mode; I am totally in the zone! But I'm usually wearing my comfy yoga pants rather than a business suit.)

In your GTZ hours, you will have a Business Lady persona. A Business Lady is a woman who makes decisions and stands behind those decisions. She carefully and tactically balances her needs and deliberately plans how she will accomplish the tasks she needs to complete.

Like the children's game Red Light, Green Light, you'll want to approach every hour in your GTZ as if you are crouching at the starting line in a ready-set-go position. You'll be establishing and maintaining a position that says, "It's *GO* time!"

I'll be the first to admit that I am guilty of starting a task, and then for some reason or another I am pulled away from that task, only to start another one, and then often another one on top of that one! It's as if I'm more concerned with movement than with purposefully finishing one task at a time. Before using this time zone concept, I found myself moving at a pace that was far too rushed. I recognized that because of my hustled and hurried pace, my focus was often way off-kilter. Sometimes I couldn't recall my original plan—if there even was one! Can you relate?

There is not necessarily anything wrong with this hiccuping or zigzagging way of working on things, but in general, it is not the best path while working in your GTZ. In your GTZ, you want to be laser focused. Like a ballerina who is spinning, around, around, and around, keeping her eyes solely focused on her focal point and never wavering. Because she is looking only at her focal point, she does not lose her balance or fall to the strong forces of her continual spins.

To locate a focal point (no ballet shoes required) when dedicating yourself to the hours in your GTZ, plan the specific and essential tasks you need to address during that time. By simply jotting down your top priorities, you'll feel prepared. You'll know you have a plan in place to work on them (even if it isn't until tomorrow).

Schedule and order your tasks by priority. Then when working in your GTZ hours, tackle your most time-sensitive tasks first. You will usually be at your prime in the beginning of your zone; capitalize on this and plan accordingly. In the GTZ, you'll be primarily working on your highest-priority tasks, especially those that have time-sensitive requirements and deadlines.

Whether your GTZ is only one power hour or as many as five or more hours of your day, make sure that you have a workable plan in place. A working plan, like a business plan, will provide you with a focal point and an order for how to best tackle your priorities. Without a plan in place prior to your GTZ hours, you'll easily fall into the ever-present trap of bouncing your way through your tasks and likely starting more tasks than you are able to complete.

Now, Business Lady, take some time to examine the various tasks on your personal or professional plate. Answer the following questions to determine which tasks should be assigned to your GTZ.

- ▶ What tasks require the most amount of your attention and focus or have time-sensitive deadlines?

- ▶ What are the essential priorities that demand a weekly time commitment?

- ▶ Which goals or to-dos should be assigned to a focused time of work?

In the green light box that follows, list your GTZ tasks—those tasks you work on when wearing your official Business Lady hat.

## GTZ Guardrails

One day, during one of our fifty required instructional driving hours, Ainsley told me that we really needed to start working on her freeway driving. Yeah, right! This was something I never, ever wanted to do! Instruct a teenager how to drive 75 miles per hour while surrounded by semitrucks and cars rushing past at fast and furious speeds? It sounded like an absolute nightmare. I tucked her request away and told her we needed to first fully master turning right on a red light and steering into the correct lane. She also told me that we needed to practice her driving in the snow so that she could drive in those conditions too. No comment.

As much as I dread the idea of my baby driving on the freeway, I love the freeway when I have a long distance to travel. Working in your GTZ is somewhat like driving on the freeway for an extended period of time. When approaching

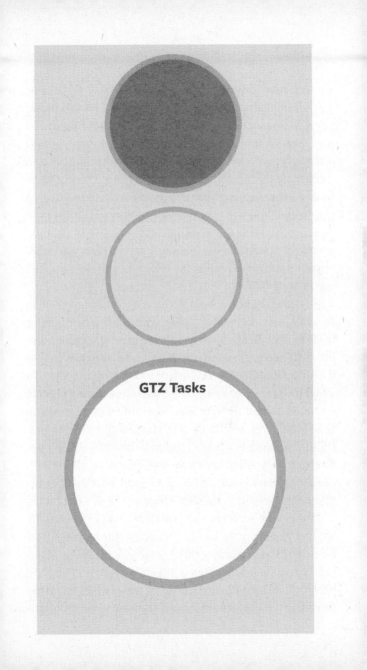

GTZ Tasks

this time zone, you are going to ease into the zone in the same way you signal and merge onto the freeway. Next, you are going to accelerate and then maintain the speed limit; you may even want to set your cruise control. You drive (work) at a steady pace, slowing down only when someone needs to merge onto the freeway or you need to change lanes. Otherwise, you are keeping your eyes on the road and regulating your speed. You will continue moving forward, in the right direction, slowing down significantly only when the time comes for you to exit the freeway. Finally, when you arrive at your destination, that is the time you will define as the end of your GTZ.

To create the best conditions for a smooth "commute" in the GTZ, first, it's helpful to have your needs in harmonious balance, specifically your emotional, mental, spiritual, and physical needs. You are not going to be very productive if you are emotionally drained or too hungry to focus. To avoid the feeling of being out of balance with your needs, consciously and thoughtfully add buffers and transition time before you shift into your constructive GTZ hours. Limit emotionally charged topics and conversations beforehand, fuel yourself with a well-balanced meal or snack, pray for a clear mind, and do something refreshing or invigorating prior to settling into your intensive work mode.

If your emotional, mental, spiritual, and physical needs are met prior to your highly productive times, you won't be as tempted to get up or stop what you are doing. Keep in mind that balancing your mind-body needs is extremely personal and individual. If you work better when snacking, then snack! Just make sure you are striving to be attuned to and aware of your needs so that unmet needs don't become distractions when you plunge into your dedicated GTZ hours. By meeting your needs prior to your GTZ hours, you will maximize your capacity and capability and you'll be better able to stay on task.

Second, when considering your GTZ, you will want to ensure that the weather and road conditions are in your favor. Setting up successful time management (increasing your levels of productivity) in your GTZ demands that your work environment be a positive and contributing force. The tasks you are working on within this time zone require you to concentrate well. If your current work space isn't conducive to your intended levels of output, it's time to make a change. Just as you might postpone a trip due to snowy road conditions, you may need to adjust your GTZ hours based on your specific daily conditions.

My current home and work duties are flexible by design—blogging, writing, organizing, and managing our home. I don't have a defined work space outside of my home, but I have discovered there are only some work-related tasks I am able to do productively at home. I can accomplish simple things such as paying bills or responding to emails at home, but for more detailed and complicated tasks—work-related and otherwise—I'm always better served to get outside of my house. I am not as focused when I try to do the high-priority tasks that fall within my GTZ hours at home. I need to get away from the dryer buzzing, the dog whining, and the counters telling me to clean them—they are so needy! It's generally too distracting for me to be productive (with my assigned

GTZ priorities) at home. This may be the exact opposite for you. The point is to identify a space where you can operate without too much distraction.

My home works extremely well for multitasking; one might even say it's ideal. (Yes, counters, dryer, and dog—I'm talking about you!) But when I need to work on an essential assignment, something that falls within my GTZ, I usually make the intentional choice to work somewhere outside my home. This is often the library or a coffee shop. When I sit down to work at an off-site location, I make a point to shut down my email app, turn my phone on silent, and spread my work stuff all over the desk or table (in other words, a surface that doesn't have jelly stuck on it from someone's breakfast bagel).

I've learned through trial and error which work spaces away from my home allow me to work more efficiently. These are my go-to spots, the places I can retreat to when I need to spend the necessary hours working on my high-priority tasks in my GTZ.

Carefully consider your work space. Is it conducive to your getting in the needed GTZ hours? It doesn't need to be a fixed spot, but it should be an area that allows you to focus. Consider everything: noise level, lighting, distractions, views, furniture, accessibility, and even the setup. Do you have everything you need in one spot? If you work in a dedicated office space, evaluate it as it relates to your specific needs. What's working? What's not working? Can you make some adjustments? Keep tweaking things until you get them just right. Do what you can to improve your work space so that you can be your most productive.

Don't fear trial and error as this is part of the process. I realize you may have limits on what you can and cannot do to your space. However, be creative and do anything and everything you can to maximize your conditions so you feel the most productive.

If you need to spend time getting your work space organized for greater productivity, I encourage you to plan an "Organize My Work Space" day. Schedule a specific time to set up your space in a way that will help you to be the most productive. Put on your old jeans, grab some cleaning supplies, plug in the shredder, say no to all work obligations, turn off your phone, and commit to revamping your work space. After this dedicated effort, you are sure to reap major dividends when it comes to your ability to concentrate and stay on task.

How you set up and organize your work space is very personal. Do what works for you. Set it up in a way that fosters and contributes to your highest levels of creativity and productivity. My preference is a neat and tidy space. I like things I'm not working on to be tucked away. I also keep several one-inch notebooks with work-related information at hand. This makes it easy for me to access the information I need while working. When I get ready to work in my GTZ, I like room to spread out, and then I get to work!

After fine-tuning your work space, consider ways you can dial out distractions or anything that may keep you from staying on task. And, yes, I know that these days it seems almost impossible to turn them all off! Like your preferred work space, your distractions may be unique to you and your situation. What is distracting to one person may not distract another, and vice versa.

When I'm working in my GTZ at a coffee shop, I'm in the habit of putting in my earbuds, sometimes even forgetting to turn on my music. There is just something about having this buffer from the noise and activity around me that helps me settle into my GTZ and not be so easily distracted.

One of the best ways to minimize unwanted interruptions is to use solid guardrails. In my GTZ, I put my phone on Do Not Disturb and shut down my email application (unless I need those specific functions for what I'm working on). Simple steps like these make a tremendous difference in what I can accomplish in a sometimes short, yet focused, amount of time.

Decide what you need to do to enforce boundaries, and then commit to keeping those boundaries in place. Doing so will boost your level of output and multiply your results.

Just as you would map out your trip, check in advance the weather conditions, and fill up your car with gas, you will want to plan, prepare, and design your environment, climate, and conditions in such a way that you are comfortable and able to do your work and do your work well. Then put on the cruise control, settle into work mode, and stay on task.

The last thing you want is to end up lost and out of gas when you are on the road to accomplishing your tasks. These hours should feel as if your time is being expanded and stretched. I want you to look forward to the hours in your GTZ and feel less stressed because you have intentionally designated time and space to work on those tasks that require the most concentration and attention. When you focus your time and energy in the GTZ, you will feel an overwhelming sense of accomplishment. Remember, this is your time to get down to business; after all, you are a Business Lady with moxie!

Following are a few questions to consider when evaluating your GTZ guardrails:

▶ Are there too many alarms, rings, beeps, or buzzes that are alerting you to nonessential interruptions?

▶ Do you need to use more clear-cut boundaries when it comes to a certain coworker or even a family member?

▶ How many times do you start and stop things? Write it down and use the data to identify what your current common distractions are. You might be surprised what you discover!

## Take the Wheel!

Now let's put your GTZ hours into your weekly schedule. Week by week you will build your three time zones into your schedule by taking each of them on an individual test drive. Going step-by-step, you will be better able to calibrate the activities that should be assigned to each time zone.

Begin by mapping out one week on your calendar, focusing only on organizing and scheduling your GTZ hours. Remember, this is the time zone you want to fiercely protect and guard. This time zone can be the most sensitive to distractions and interruptions, so be sure to consider this reality when allocating your blocks of time.

The number of hours in your GTZ will be unique to you and based on your lifestyle. Your work, home, and life requirements will be the deciding factors for how many hours to allocate to this time zone. You may have only one GTZ block listed daily, or you may have as many as three or four. You might even have a day or many days that don't allow for any GTZ hours.

Mark your GTZ hours and tasks on either your personal calendar or the weekly schedule that follows. Per your productivity chart (chap. 3), first fill in the times in the left-hand column at which you circled three stars. These are your GTZ hours, your most productive times of the day. Then, referring to the green light box, distribute the tasks you listed into the GTZ time blocks for each day of the week.

After assigning and using your GTZ times and activities for one week, step back and see if your allocations of time were captured correctly. Analyze whether what you planned and scheduled was realized. Consider the following questions as you measure your progress:

▸ Were you able to protect your GTZ hours?

▸ How were your productivity levels in your GTZ?

▸ Did you have too few (or too many) hours dedicated to your GTZ?

This was your introduction to mapping out successful GTZ hours on your weekly schedule. This was only a test run. Don't worry if you got halfway through the week and

# Weekly Schedule: GTZ

| Time | Sunday | Monday | Tuesday | Wednesday | Thursday | Friday | Saturday |
|------|--------|--------|---------|-----------|----------|--------|----------|
|      |        |        |         |           |          |        |          |
|      |        |        |         |           |          |        |          |
|      |        |        |         |           |          |        |          |
|      |        |        |         |           |          |        |          |
|      |        |        |         |           |          |        |          |
|      |        |        |         |           |          |        |          |
|      |        |        |         |           |          |        |          |
|      |        |        |         |           |          |        |          |

forgot about your GTZ hours! You are working to form a new habit in time management, and yes, this too takes time.

Appropriately and adequately planned hours in your GTZ will enable you to consistently achieve your highest and essential priorities. By using your moxie attitude, best Business Lady demeanor, and the necessary guardrails, you will be able to step on the gas when the light turns green and go for it!

Now I'm off to apply some calming essential oils and say another protective prayer as I hand over my car keys to my precious—and now licensed—teen driver.

### Tip—Five Ways to Supercharge Your Week

Supercharge your week by choosing one day a week to do the following. You will be better prepared and will have more time to work and focus in your GTZ hours.

- *Plan your breakfast menu*. Have a plan for your daily breakfast. This way you can shop according to the plan, and your family will know what they can choose from during the week. I try to create self-serve options as much as possible. We've even followed themes for different days of the week (Waffle Wednesdays, Toast & Fruit Thursdays, etc.).
- *Plan your lunch menu*. By prepping veggies and fruit, stocking lunch and snack bins, and preparing any main dish items ahead of time (such as pastas, sandwiches, or soups), you'll create more time during the morning rush. Prepackaging all of your lunches for the week can be a game changer!

▶ *Plan your dinner menu.* Designate how many nights you will eat in and how many nights you will eat out, considering any activities already on your weekly schedule, and plan a menu for the week. Also, make note of any meals or sides you need to prepare for upcoming events and, like your lunch menu, look for ways to prepare things ahead of time.

▶ *Plan your daily outfits.* For kids and adults alike, planning out your outfits in advance can be a super time-saver, especially on early school or workday mornings. Consider mapping out a week of outfits. Coordinate clothing ahead of time, try on the outfits, and make sure everything is ironed and ready to wear.

▶ *Plan your schedule.* Look at your week ahead and make a point to know the key items already scheduled and to anticipate any others that may pop up. Communicate the weekly schedule to all family members, and keep your calendar updated.

> Take back your time—
> GREEN means go!

# 5

# Your Yellow
# Time Zone (YTZ)

## Flex Time

Juggling is an illusion. . . . In reality, the balls are being
independently caught and thrown in rapid succession.
. . . It is actually task switching.

Gary Keller

n your GTZ, you work on your most focused tasks. Your
Yellow Time Zone (YTZ) is when you will work on several simpler tasks at the same time. In both zones, you
work on priority tasks; however, the main difference is the
level of attention your tasks require of you. In your YTZ,
you will intentionally choose those tasks that allow for
fluidity and the potential for starting and stopping points.
Your YTZ hours will be flexible. If you hear an alert, you

can respond. If you are interrupted, you will have the time and space to reply.

Sometimes the hours in your YTZ will be supercharged and other times super mellow. Allow me to warn you though. Just like when you approach a yellow traffic light, in the YTZ you must *proceed with caution*. It is tempting to try to squeeze too many activities into your YTZ, which can result in an underutilization of your time. It is often tougher to navigate the YTZ than the other time zones *because* of the flexibility in the YTZ. You must capitalize on the flexibility of the zone to maximize your effectiveness.

One Friday morning while in my YTZ, I set out for the grocery store for our weekly food haul—feeding my family of five. As I was grabbing my shopping cart, placing my purse in the child seat, and tucking my chai tea latte into a spot where it would be able to sustain any sudden movements without spilling, I overheard a woman speaking loudly into her phone. She had two children strapped into her cart and appeared to be on a customer-service type of call. She was obviously frustrated with the status of how things were going (or not), and I immediately felt empathy for what she was experiencing.

Haven't we all been there? We just want to make a quick phone call to resolve a small issue, but instead the phone call goes on and on and the resolution appears to be nowhere in sight. This overwhelmed woman was in this position. She wasn't getting the results she wanted or the help she needed.

As I pushed my cart forward, her frustrated dialogue continued with an increase in volume. Then, out of nowhere, it became obvious that she had lost the connection with her call. Visibly angry, she proceeded to make an even bigger scene, at which point I moved on.

Strolling through the store, I processed what I had just witnessed. As I put in my earbuds, selected a podcast, and started to load up fruits and veggies into my cart, I had an aha moment. By attempting to make an important phone call, this woman (God bless her, I've been her) had decided to do a GTZ task in her YTZ. She chose a mismatched combination of tasks—making a lengthy phone call while grocery shopping with her children. These weren't complementary tasks; they were competing tasks.

Making a phone call *can* work during a shopping trip (and maybe even with kids), but a time-intensive, emotionally charged, and connection-dependent phone call is always better scheduled within the GTZ. In the YTZ, proceed with caution, use wisdom, and be discerning about which tasks you choose to combine and multitask. The right combination can and will make all the difference.

## Multitasking

When working within your flex time, your YTZ, you need to learn how to juggle and multitask your work tasks in a productive manner. This time zone is likely when you will be interrupted the most often; therefore, choose the tasks that can most easily be paused if required.

When I think of the word *multitasking*, I'm immediately reminded of the movie *Sweet Home Alabama*. In a scene in the movie, the main character, played by Reese Witherspoon, is talking to her mother on the phone. During their phone conversation, her mother comments to Reese's character that she is doing two things at once. Her mother clarifies that she is talking on the phone while also peeling potatoes, and then goes on to say, "Oprah calls it multitasking."[1]

I'm sure we can both agree that Oprah knows a thing or two about multitasking.

Often multitasking gets a bad rap. I saw a quote by Steve Uzelle that sums up what it feels like for many of us: "The opportunity to screw up more than one thing at a time."[2] Multitasking can be a strength or a weakness. Sometimes, rather than multiplying our time, we multiply only the potential number of mistakes we make.

There is a productive way to multitask and an unproductive way to multitask. Knowing the correct way will make the difference between experiencing more stress or more success in your YTZ. The productive way to multitask is to schedule the appropriate balance of two (or more) tasks together. *Successful multitasking relies heavily on choosing the right combination of tasks to work on at the same time*. With the right balance, you'll get more done without compromising your level of quality. Your quantity of time will become time that is well spent.

Multitasking should be attempted only when it allows you to reap more benefit and reward from your efforts. When you can accomplish more in less time and, most importantly, keep your mistakes to a minimum, multitasking can be appropriate.

There is a concept that teaches it is better to do only one thing at a time. To which I say yes—some of the time!

There are many tasks, however, that can easily be done in partnership with others on your to-do list. In your YTZ, you'll want to intentionally choose those smaller and simpler responsibilities, the ones that don't require 100 percent of your attention. These tasks are your nonessential, less time-sensitive tasks in comparison to those you assigned to your GTZ. The YTZ tasks allow space to adjust, stop, and restart when necessary.

In my YTZ, I like to combine different types of tasks, such as a relational activity with a practical one. For example, I'll ask a friend to take a walk with me. This satisfies a relational need by spending time together and a practical need by taking care of my health. Or I will combine a physical activity with a mental one. I'll create time to clean up our basement while I listen to an audiobook. This way I can enjoy a book while moving around and getting things more organized. Matching together certain tasks makes my YTZ hours count double! When you pair a mindful task with a mindless task, it results in you being a successful multitasker.

On the flip side, when I do a poor job of choosing the right combination of tasks to work on in my YTZ hours, I usually get less done. For example, I've been guilty of trying to read and respond to a detailed email while also attempting to listen to one of my children tell me something important about their day. As I'm half listening to my sweet kiddo, I'm also sending off an email response that has numerous typos because I wasn't giving it my full attention. Then my child proceeds to ask me a question from their daily download that I don't know how to answer because

I was only half listening. And let's face it, half listening is basically not listening, and half of doing anything results in half of the result at best.

When I find myself in the middle of a poor choice for my time zone, I'm confronted with the fact that I'm not making the most of my time. Instead, I'm doing a terrible job of multitasking. I'm not working smarter, I'm only working harder, and I'm not multiplying anything. I'm minimizing my effectiveness and wasting too much energy. The better choice would be to fully engage with and listen to my child's account of their day while working on something that requires much less of my attention and focus. A more complementary task might be unloading the dishwasher or wiping down the kitchen counter.

When you choose tasks that complement each other in your YTZ, your YTZ hours will be much more productive. Picking tasks that require less of your attention and then combining them with complementary ones is the best recipe for productivity success!

In her book *Bittersweet*, Shauna Niequist writes, "I love the illusion of being able to do it all, and I'm fascinated with people who seem to do that, who have challenging careers and beautiful homes and vibrant minds and well-tended abs. Throw in polite children and a garden, and I'm coming over for lessons."[3] She goes on to talk about how she created a "Things I Do" list and a "Things I Don't Do" list. I love this! I think we should have similar lists!

The more you keep the spotlight on the purpose for your season of life and what you are called to be and do, the more intentional your YTZ will be. If you are certain of the things you don't do (which can be anything), you'll be able to better manage the flexibility of your YTZ with the things you do.

You won't be tempted to start sewing your own clothes if you've already written *sewing* on your Things I Don't Do list. Or if you are like me and you've written on your list that you don't make your bed (Shauna wrote this one on her list; another reason why I love her!), you don't need to add this to your to-do list or to your YTZ.

Proceed with caution in your YTZ, and don't do things just because you are supposed to or because others expect you to. Know what you will do and what you won't do. Then choose only those items on your Things I Do list for your YTZ, and if multitasking, make sure they complement each other.

## Juggling Lady

A great visual image for multitasking is a juggler keeping three balls moving in the air simultaneously. The reason they are able to juggle the balls is because they have learned how to balance the movement between them. There is a fluidity of movement between the three balls. All three are receiving the juggler's equal attention, though not full attention. Each is getting a third of the juggler's attention—at all times.

A juggler is not frantically trying to keep all their balls in the air. For them, it's a dance and a rhythm. They are able to anticipate the changes in movement and are not surprised by unexpected interruptions. They are flexible, able to go with the flow and keep things moving.

When you multitask, you are shifting your attention between multiple tasks, hence the prefix *multi*. Therefore, choosing those tasks that require only a percentage of your attention will make your juggling successful. Balancing smaller tasks within smaller pockets of time is an intentional strategy to help you get more things done throughout your day. When you effectively use this strategy, you will become a Juggling Lady!

I'm able to juggle some of my smaller duties simultaneously when I'm making dinner in the late afternoon or early evening. Though this is often the craziest time of my day because we're all reentering our home from long days at school and work, it is also when I'm able to multitask with ease. I can easily start and stop things as required. I can move from small task to small task. I've intentionally built in margin for interruptions.

While dinner is simmering on the stove, I'm able to quickly reorganize a cupboard, fill out a permission form, go through the mail, or do a quick cleanup of the great room. I can do this because cooking one of my go-to recipes doesn't require my full attention. However, this is not the case if I'm making a new recipe for the first time or preparing a full dinner menu for guests.

An easy way to think about using the time in your YTZ is to break it down into ten-to-fifteen-minute increments and to consider the task at hand. There are many small tasks: switching a load of laundry, filing away a few pieces of paper, putting something away where it belongs, deleting old photos off your phone, decluttering a desk drawer, writing a thank-you note. Each of these can be accomplished in fifteen minutes or less. Look for these types of activities on your to-do list and work them into your YTZ hours. Coordinating small tasks with other simple tasks will result in your accomplishing more in less time.

I like to multitask while grocery shopping. I put in my earbuds and listen to a podcast. This enables me to fill my time with some positive inspiration and information while also checking items off my grocery list. This combination feeds my family and my soul. Or I may multitask when I'm home chatting on the phone. I use the speaker function and fold laundry, prep food, or dust at the same time. Or when I'm taking my kids to and from sports practices, I make a point to bring along a book. This way, while I'm waiting at the field or pool, I can use the time to also catch up on some reading.

By remaining intentional within my YTZ, I'm able to accomplish multiple tasks. Two or three effortless items can easily be juggled together, especially when I plan accordingly and in advance.

I've never been able to successfully juggle like a juggler, but I have learned how to juggle multiple tasks, and I love the feeling it produces. I feel relieved and rewarded for my efforts. When I can knock out those smaller to-do items, keep things organized, and get more done, my stress level lowers and I feel more at peace.

When you select tasks that fit well together for your YTZ, you will be a Juggling Lady, able to keep everything moving successfully. This will help you to maximize both the quality *and* quantity of your time! By coordinating the right choices of activities at the right times, you'll get more done every time.

Following are some questions to consider as you think about the various duties you work on each day that might naturally fall into your YTZ:

- ▶ What sorts of tasks would be good options to assign to your YTZ?
- ▶ Which of your assignments needs less of your focus?
- ▶ What responsibilities might work well in tandem?

In the yellow light box that follows, list your YTZ tasks—those tasks you could work on while wearing your stylish Juggling Lady hat.

## YTZ Guardrails

In your YTZ, your time will more resemble a short drive to and from work or shuffling your kids around in a carpool or being stuck in stop-and-go traffic. You will have the ability to start and stop things with greater ease. You won't need to turn off all of your alerts and notifications. However, you should still consider what guardrails to put in place so you can carefully juggle the multiple tasks you assign to your YTZ.

Improved technology, like smartphones and laptops, provides us with greater flexibility and an even greater ability to multitask. Before I had a smartphone, I would sit down at our oversized computer monitor, usually only once a day, to get caught up on emails. Nowadays I find

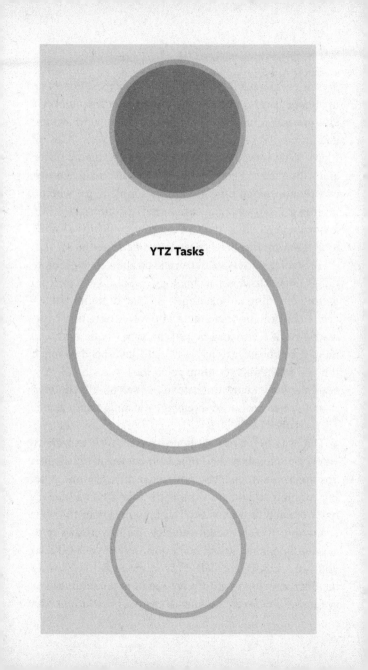

**YTZ Tasks**

myself checking and replying to emails almost hourly on my phone, simply because it's much easier and quicker. I also remember having to type in an address on MapQuest and print out a paper copy of driving directions. Now all I have to do is type the address into the app on my phone and within ten seconds (or less) I know the optimal route, exactly how much time it will take for me to get where I need to go, and what the current traffic patterns are. Talk about a time savings! (If only someone could drive for me too—oh wait, I have a licensed teenage driver now.)

Technological advances can and do allow us to get more things done. However, technology can also keep us from getting anything done, simply because of unlimited access to information and the reality of information overload. I know I've asked myself this type of question—on more than one occasion: "How did I just spend so much time on Instagram/googling celebrities' vacation photos/searching new homes for sale in our neighborhood (even though we're not house shopping)/watching funny videos on YouTube?"

One way to guard your hours in your YTZ, especially when it comes to technology, is to be sensitive to when you might need to pivot or move into a different time zone. For example, if you are working in your YTZ and finally receive that return phone call that requires your full concentration, you are faced with a choice. If you choose to answer the phone, it will be best to shift to your GTZ so you can focus on the call. This might look like closing the door, moving to a different room, or communicating to family, coworkers, or friends that you need to take an important phone call. If instead you choose to let the call go to voicemail, you can plan a time in your GTZ to respond to the call. The key to success in each time zone is knowing when to shift or change zones to best address what is in front of you.

When it comes to monitoring technology usage, the problem for both adults and children alike is that our smartphones have become our own personal handheld minicomputers. They have replaced several devices, which have been combined into one. You no longer need a separate camera, digital reader, desktop computer, or TV. Smartphones can be all these things and much, much more. And because they contain so much of our information—from contacts to communication to calendars—we are looking at them all the time. They are a one-stop shop for information and entertainment, not necessarily in that order.

One afternoon as I was staring down at my phone, my son came into the kitchen and asked me if I knew how to check the amount of time I spend on my phone. He was referring specifically to how much time I spend on the various applications on my phone. I told him that I didn't know, because I'm technologically challenged or lazy—or both. Right then and there, he showed me how to check my hourly usage per week per application under the settings on my phone. Thanks, I think?

Connor wanted to know for himself how much time he was spending on his phone. When he saw his usage, broken into hours per application, he felt challenged to make better choices with regard to his phone and time management. I too was reluctantly convicted. I may have said something like, "Hey bud, why did you have to show me this feature? I think I liked it better when I was in denial about how much time I spend staring at my phone." Ignorance truly can be blissful.

It was a bit shocking to see the total number of hours I had spent on Pinterest in just one week. It was something like fifty-one hours—I'm kidding. But it *was* eye-opening to see the number of hours per week I was spending scrolling, searching, and surfing. I knew this did not reflect the best use of my time.

While technology provides convenience and is a time-saver, it can *also* be a serious time thief! If we are not careful with our technology usage (how, when, and why we use it), our devices can keep us from being the productive multitaskers we were born to be and rob us of our potential.

As you think about your YTZ hours, consider how you are using technology in order to save time and how you might be wasting time by using technology. Technology will play an important role in your YTZ hours and will help you to multitask. But be careful that the conveniences don't take away from your ability to remain productive and get things done.

Just as technology can affect our ability to accomplish things, people too can make it tough for us to get things done. When I worked as a human resources manager, I was the office go-to person. I had a door to my office, but the door was rarely shut. Running an HR department for a company of 125 employees meant that when a new hire didn't show up for their first shift, I was the first one to receive a phone call. Or when someone's paycheck wasn't ready, they came looking for me. If performance reviews and pay raises needed to be discussed, I was the one consulted. But most of all, I was a sounding board for every employee.

Because of my open-door policy and the frequent interruptions, I learned to save my more-focused tasks for the least-disruptive times in my day. It took daily discipline, but it was necessary in order for me to complete my top priorities. I also set up some gentle boundaries where and when I could to protect my GTZ whenever possible.

Working in an office environment can be one of the biggest challenges to time management. Much of the workday can feel more like flex or interrupted time. You may find that some days you barely had five to ten minutes to focus on any one thing. You likely can't change everything about this reality, but you can be aware of it and look for ways to creatively work around it.

Maybe come in early one morning each week to get ahead of the noise and distractions. Or occasionally take a long lunch break and work on things while at lunch. Or you might need to have a specific conversation with a certain someone who tends to chat with you more than you have time for. Oftentimes, when we address some of the interruptions that are affecting our ability to be productive and put up some necessary guardrails, we can help to minimize the frequency and effect of those interruptions.

Your job by nature may demand that you be in flex-time mode most of the time. If this is the case, you can still learn how best to juggle the demands of your job and match tasks with times in order to be more productive. It might not be a perfect arrangement, but it can be better. Just remember, if you know you are in your YTZ, just like in stop-and-go traffic you will eventually get there!

Following are a few questions to consider when evaluating your YTZ guardrails:

- ► How do you set aside your GTZ tasks when you need to deliberately stay in your YTZ?

- ► Do you use boundaries for how much time you spend on your devices—phone, computer, TV?

- ► Consider the times in your day when you are most often interrupted. Are there some changes you can implement to help make these times more fruitful?

## Take the Wheel!

Now it's time to take one week and prioritize your YTZ hours. You are going to highlight only this zone for one week to learn how best to implement the YTZ into your schedule.

This time zone will help you get more done within smaller windows of time in your day. Start to look at your commute time as a productive time. Begin to use waiting time as a time to get a few things done. Think of the times when you have less scheduled or a smaller window of time as opportunities to work on some of your simpler tasks.

Thinking off the top of your head, you probably already know the times when you multitask well—those time slots during your daily schedule when you are able to work on more than one activity at a time and remain productive while also allowing for interruptions. This time zone is often one you'll find naturally sprinkled throughout your day. Sometimes it may be only five minutes here and there, but you'll learn to recognize when you are in your YTZ and how to make this an increasingly productive time.

Walk the dog while you return a phone call—done. Get in a quick treadmill run during your lunch break while you listen to your favorite podcast—done. Catch up on your favorite TV show while you finish folding laundry—done. Combine three of your errands into one trip and complete all three—done.

Use your YTZ to combine activities, whether relational and practical or physical and mental. No matter the activities, strive to combine those tasks that complement each other and work for you.

When you begin to organize the specific hours that you will assign to your YTZ, look for those pockets of time in your day that naturally support flexibility and fluidity. This time zone is where you may be inclined to take on too much simply because of the design of the zone. Learn to know yourself and how you best multitask. Evaluate which tasks in your life are the most conducive to multitasking and incorporate these into this time zone. It's OK if you initially misalign activities. Once you recognize that this has happened, learn from it and commit to making a better choice next time. Remain consistent about this, and I promise it will start to click.

Your YTZ hours may range from as little as one or two hours per day to as many as eight or more. Your YTZ hours will most likely be scheduled into every day, but this is your time—don't feel like you have to follow any specific set of rules.

Mark your YTZ hours and tasks on either your personal calendar or the weekly schedule that follows. Per your productivity chart (chap. 3), first fill in the times in the left-hand column at which you circled two stars. These are your YTZ hours. Then, referring to the yellow light box, distribute the tasks you listed into the YTZ time blocks for each day of the week.

Like with your GTZ, after one week of using your YTZ hours in your schedule, step back and see how you did. This was your test drive of your YTZ! Consider the following questions when reflecting on your YTZ:

► Were you able to plan your YTZ hours successfully and keep them separate from your GTZ hours?

► Where do you need to make some adjustments with your YTZ scheduling?

► Did you have too few (or too many) hours dedicated to your YTZ?

In your YTZ, remember to do your best to be a successful Juggling Lady, creating the right conditions for your YTZ. You should tweak and adjust as you work through this zone. There is a lot of elasticity in this zone, so don't feel like you have to look at things through an all-or-nothing lens. How you modify your flex time is going to be personal to you.

We all have different strengths and abilities. As we work to combine the right tasks into our scheduled YTZ hours,

## Weekly Schedule: YTZ

| Time | Sunday | Monday | Tuesday | Wednesday | Thursday | Friday | Saturday |
|------|--------|--------|---------|-----------|----------|--------|----------|
|      |        |        |         |           |          |        |          |
|      |        |        |         |           |          |        |          |
|      |        |        |         |           |          |        |          |
|      |        |        |         |           |          |        |          |
|      |        |        |         |           |          |        |          |
|      |        |        |         |           |          |        |          |
|      |        |        |         |           |          |        |          |
|      |        |        |         |           |          |        |          |
|      |        |        |         |           |          |        |          |
|      |        |        |         |           |          |        |          |
|      |        |        |         |           |          |        |          |
|      |        |        |         |           |          |        |          |
|      |        |        |         |           |          |        |          |

we are able to successfully finish many of our simpler assignments—despite the numerous interruptions to our time!

Now it's time for me to head out on yet another trip to the grocery store. I've downloaded my latest favorite podcast, created my shopping list, and even remembered to load the reusable sacks into the car. (Chances are I'll forget them in the car, but hey, at least I try!) This Juggling Lady is ready to shop! And if there's time, I may even pick up a Redbox movie and fill up the car with gas in preparation for a full weekend.

If only someone would magically show up to help me unload the groceries and put them away. . . . A girl can dream, can't she?

### Tip—Five Ways to Tame Technology

Keep technology the time-saver it was designed to be. Try the following to better organize your technology and realize increased productivity.

- *Keep fewer apps.* Delete apps from your phone and/or devices that aren't benefiting you. While it can be convenient to check on things throughout your day, this can easily become a distraction, keeping you from the things you need to focus on.

- *Use Washi Tape.* Minimize confusion over which earbuds or phone charger belongs to whom by using a different colored Washi Tape for each family member's devices. Labeling things individually will make it less likely that the wrong pair of earbuds will be snatched during the morning rush.

▶ *Set Do Not Disturb*. Use the Do Not Disturb feature on your phone or device to put boundaries around your time. Doing so will help to safeguard those hours you want to dedicate to more focused and meaningful work or activities. You do not have to be available 24/7!

▶ *Create a device basket*. A device basket in your home can be used to collect devices when not being used. Silence the alerts and ring tones to help minimize interruptions. Using a tool like this helps all of us (parents and children alike) to remember to set down our devices from time to time.

▶ *Schedule more*. Commit to establishing some time frames around checking your email, looking at your social media accounts, and so on. You'll be more productive if you set up parameters for how often you take part in these activities. Deliberately close applications that are prone to causing disruptions, and allow only alerts that help you to stay on track of your commitments and your time. Set a timer for when you want to check these things versus checking every five minutes. This will help you save time and be more productive.

---

Take back your time—
YELLOW means proceed
with caution!

---

# 6

# Your Red
# Time Zone (RTZ)

## Fill Time

My favorite things in life don't cost any money. It's
really clear that the most precious resource we all have
is time.

Steve Jobs

**P**roductive people make time to consistently recharge.
Productive people value their *stop* time. As a result,
they are able to reap the rewards of extraordinary
productivity. For you to have *go* time, you must also have
*stop* time.

Our mode of life today—constant stress, poor diet, lack of
exercise and sleep—leads to what scientists call *exhaustion
syndrome*. The rest of us call it *burnout*. We continually

push through each day, postponing the renewal time our brains and bodies need. . . .

By contrast, extraordinarily productive people consistently recharge. They have a more constant feeling of energy and capability throughout the day.[1]

Now that you've assigned your focused tasks to your GTZ and your flexible tasks to your YTZ, it's time to examine your Red Time Zone (RTZ). Your RTZ is the time you dedicate to your personal restoration. It is your fill time. Your RTZ hours are when you apply the brakes, come to a complete stop, and reboot. Think of your RTZ time like filling up your car's gas tank or scheduling a regular maintenance check. Your schedule needs to include the quality and quantity of time required to maintain you! You need "me" time!

If you don't spend adequate time recharging your batteries, your hours in your GTZ and YTZ will be less fruitful. Your RTZ is the foundation for your GTZ and YTZ. When you schedule and protect the necessary time for renewal and find ways to fill your tank, you will avoid running on fumes in your other two zones. Running on fumes is the least productive way to complete what you most need to accomplish.

When I ran my first half marathon, I found myself running on fumes. I turned thirty-five that year and decided it would be a good idea to train for a race. I had not run a half marathon before, and it seemed like a great fitness goal. Committed to the concept, I signed up, printed off a running schedule, and began race training.

Looking back, I give myself a C+ for my training efforts. By the day of the race, I had done only about half of the recommended training runs. I justified my lack of training by telling myself, *I've run a 10K (6.2 miles), and a half marathon is only two 10Ks combined. So how hard can a half marathon be?* Famous last words.

The morning of the race, I woke up at the crack of dawn and ate a banana before David and I set out for the race in downtown Portland. When it began, I started off confident and felt fantastic! I settled into my pace feeling grateful for the cool spring weather and the clear blue skies. As I effortlessly ran up the first gentle hill, I decided I wouldn't drink any water offered to me along the race route. I thought it would be too hard to run while drinking from a tiny cup, and I also didn't want to have to slow down.

My first seven miles went well, and I was able to maintain my pace and run with relative ease. In my mind, I thought, *My first 10K is done!* Then around mile eight things abruptly changed. I felt as though I could barely lift up my feet. My legs were becoming heavier and heavier, making it almost impossible for me to continue running.

Suddenly, I felt as though I had absolutely no energy left, and I still had five more miles to run! Running on fumes, I was exhausted and overwhelmed but was still determined to finish the race—no matter what.

Please note, this was not the normal midcourse feelings I had experienced in previous races. This wasn't an annoying side ache or a typical muscle pain. This was different. I was barely able to move my body forward. I was weak all over and had absolutely no energy left. My tank was completely empty.

I forced myself with all of the will I could muster to continue running (or shuffling) despite the fact that it felt almost impossible. In a complete daze, I crossed the finish line and found David, who was thrilled with his race results. Apparently, he had eaten more than a banana before the race and had taken advantage of the various beverages and snacks provided along the race route. I had done the exact opposite. I had not eaten enough for breakfast and had not kept my body fueled throughout the race. I exerted a ton of effort and energy while extremely dehydrated and undernourished.

After finishing my shuffle, all I wanted to do was sit down (or faint) and try to stop the pain. I could hardly walk at this point, and my body was shaking from head to toe. I learned, while lying curled up in a ball, that I was experiencing what runners refer to as bonking. *Bonking* is defined as "a sudden and overwhelming feeling of running out of energy. . . . With heavy legs, a body-wide feeling of fatigue and sometimes dizziness, you are forced to stop."[2]

I had bonked.

Bonking is what happens when you don't adequately prepare and train for the hours you have dedicated to your green and yellow time zones. If you don't sufficiently fuel your body beforehand, you won't have enough fuel in your tank to continue moving forward and be productive. Consequently, you may be less productive or forced to stop altogether.

It took several hours, lots of rehydration, and appropriate nutrition after the race to feel normal again. I made a commitment from that point on to better prepare for any future races. I had not prioritized and protected my physical needs prior to the race, and this resulted in suffering unhealthy and uncomfortable consequences. I finished the race, but I didn't finish well. My results were less than I desired; my poor planning led to a poor result.

To avoid bonking or burnout, you must create time for renewal. To be better prepared for the demands on your time and energy, it is imperative to commit to *making time* for yourself. To keep your energy tank filled, you need to prioritize your fill time—your time to just be.

## Maintenance

Fill time is when you are taking care of your personal needs in the moment. Your personal maintenance is your "me" time. Like scheduling maintenance appointments for your car, I encourage you to schedule appointments (time) for your personal maintenance. When you do, you are equipping your body to run well. Regular maintenance is important not only for your physical being but also for all the other parts of your being.

During fill time in your RTZ, you may be addressing your emotional, mental, spiritual, or physical needs. Fill time is when you come to a complete stop—whatever "stop" looks like to you. You create the time to fill up your tank so that when you need to move again, you are ready to go.

In your RTZ, you shift from doing to being. Your fill time is for those interests and hobbies you look forward to. Consider the types of things you gravitate toward that help you to experience a sense of renewal. Think about what choices you make that allow you to apply your brakes or press the reset button. The activities you assign to your RTZ will be exclusive and specific to you. You may still be productive in your RTZ; however, your investment of time should result in the feeling of restoration rather than the need for rest! Your fill time can be anything you find relaxing. It's whatever you want to do in your "me" time.

My fill time looks like one-on-one time with a friend, picking up a chai tea latte from a drive-thru coffee shop, taking my dog for a walk, or curling up on the couch with a cozy blanket and a good book. It's the relaxing time I get to spend watching TV after a long organizing appointment, the refreshing time I set aside for an exercise class before a jam-packed day, or the restorative time I dedicate to my bimonthly hair appointment. It can even be tasks such as reorganizing my closet, painting a room, or sewing a pair of curtains. All of these activities feel like self-care to me, and they help me to press my reset button.

*Your self-care (maintenance) is anything you do for yourself!*

When I miss a maintenance appointment for myself, my body (emotionally, mentally, spiritually, or physically) is impacted in a negative way. I may feel more tired than usual or my stress level may skyrocket or a tension head-ache may attack. While each of these things may occur from time to time, I know they can usually be avoided if I make the purposeful choice to safeguard time for self-care. I've learned the hard way that I don't want to be running on fumes, hoping I make it to the gas station in time. I want to make time in my weekly schedule to fuel up, especially before the gas light comes on. When I do, I am better able to minimize my stress level. By maintaining me, I am better able to *be* me.

Intentionally scheduling the time needed for your personal maintenance is what helps you to take better care of yourself and others. Remember, your maintenance is personal, just like you. You are your own year, style, make, and model.

## Nurturing Lady

As women, we can tend to put our own needs last. We are hardwired to be nurturers. While this is a wonderful trait, it often means we don't leave adequate time for our own personal restoration.

In your RTZ, you are going to set down your focused Business Lady hat and your flexible Juggling Lady hat and put on your Nurturing Lady hat. This is the hat that will help you to renew. When you wear your Nurturing Lady hat, you'll be committing to only those tasks that involve taking care of *you*. You'll look and plan for ways to nurture yourself through the kind of self-care activities that enable you to recharge. God designed you to rest, and it's important to honor that part of how God made you.

Think of your RTZ hours as the Sabbath hours within your schedule. God doesn't want us running on fumes for six days only to crash and burn on the seventh day. He wants us to strike a balance day in and day out between doing and being. At the end of each day in the creation story, God reflected on what he had made and said it was "good." We need to take time to do the same.

Self-care is a fundamental need we often overlook, which then leads to burnout. If you want to become a more productive person, you must become comfortable wearing your Nurturing Lady hat. There are many different styles of Nurturing Lady hats. Choose the hat style that most fits your personal style.

It could be that you envision heading to the day spa for your preferred kind of treatment. When you arrive and check in, you immediately feel a sense of calm. You hear the soft, mellow music and smell the aromatherapy candle's scent, and you can't help but feel like slowing down and coming to a complete stop. They offer you a fuzzy bathrobe, warm slippers, and a tall glass of cucumber water. You are able to set down your personal belongings and relax. You are provided with the time to sit, to be, and to rest.

It could be that you envision going to the gym for your favorite exercise dance class. You swipe your membership card, fill up your water bottle, grab a workout towel, and make your way to the studio. You love to dance. You feel free when you dance. You are able to let go when you dance. You enter the room, catch up with a few friends, and find your regular spot. You get to be, you get to let go, and you get to be free.

It could be that you envision leisurely preparing your favorite recipe on a Saturday afternoon. You find cooking a wonderful way to unwind. You put on your favorite music and pour your favorite beverage. You take your time and move slowly. You slice and mix the delicious ingredients and enjoy the wonderful aromas that fill your kitchen. You feel energized and inspired by being able to create artistic and colorful dishes. When the meal is ready, you savor it and cherish reconnecting with your loved ones.

When you don your Nurturing Lady hat, whatever shape or style best suits you, you are generating time for your restoration. You may prefer taking a nap, jogging, curling up with a book in front of a fire, getting a pedicure, gardening, or taking an art class. What is key is that the activities you choose for your fill time satisfy your need for self-care. They help you to personally feel restored, refreshed, and renewed.

There are no right or wrong activities when it comes to what you assign to the hours in your RTZ. The only guideline is that your choices must fall under your personal definition of what is self-care for you. Six categories to consider are refueling (eating), refreshing (exercising), relating (connecting), relaxing (hobbies), resting (sleeping), and restoring (personal care). All six areas are necessary for self-care. Consider the following questions and identify which of these categories need an increased amount of time dedicated to them to better prepare for your RTZ:

▶ Refueling—Are you eating the right types of foods? Do you eat at regular times? Are there foods you would like to eat more or less of?

▶ Refreshing—What types of physical activities help you recharge and get moving? Which forms of exercise would you like to spend more time doing? What helps you to feel refreshed when it comes to different types of physical movement?

▶ Relating—How do you like to connect with others? Which primary relationships help you to feel connected and cared about? What types of social settings do you prefer?

▶ Relaxing—What hobbies do you *love* to do? Which activities would you like to spend more time on? What is a hobby you have always wanted to try but haven't made time for?

▶ Resting—Are you getting the adequate rest your body needs? Do you wake up feeling refreshed? How do you feel during the day—energized or exhausted?

▶ Restoring—Are you making time for a regular haircut, a manicure, or something that makes you feel more put together? Do you often feel rushed when needing to get ready in the morning? If so, is there a change you could make to help this time be more restorative?

Keeping in mind all six categories, now consider some of the options you could assign to your RTZ time. Use the following questions to help you identify activities that recharge you and should be listed in your RTZ:

▶ What activities energize you?

▶ What do you look forward to spending your time doing in your downtime?

▶ How do you define self-care for yourself?

In the red light box that follows, list any and all RTZ options for yourself.

Laura Vanderkam, author of *I Know How She Does It*, shares this about self-care: "If you want to make the pieces of life fit together, if you want to build a career, raise a family, and stay sane, it is hard to escape the conclusion that self-care is the secret ingredient. Sleep, exercise, and leisure time are glorious things."[3] When you determine the ways that help you to find "fill" in your RTZ, you will not only be increasingly productive in your GTZ and YTZ but—and the best part—you will also be protecting your health. When you don't make time for your own restoration, you will not be able to do all that God is calling you to do. We all have a need for rest. Don't ignore this basic need; you want to avoid bonking at all costs!

Commit to wearing your Nurturing Lady hat with confidence, knowing that for every minute you dedicate to self-care, you will experience a positive ripple effect of increased energy, stamina, and productivity in your focus and flex times.

## RTZ Guardrails

It's important to think of the RTZ as a priority zone that requires the same level of attention as the other time zones. Sarah Young writes in her book *Jesus Calling*:

Learn to unwind whenever possible, resting in the Presence of your Shepherd. This electronic age keeps My children

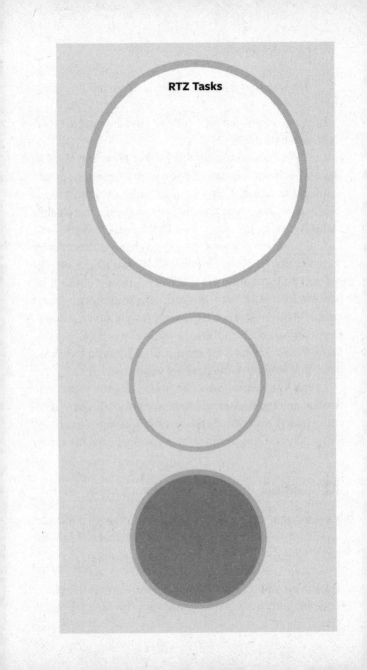

RTZ Tasks

"wired" much of the time, too tense to find Me in the midst of their moments. I built into your very being the need for rest. How twisted the world has become when people feel guilty about meeting this basic need! How much time and energy they waste by being always on the go, rather than taking time to seek My direction for their lives.[4]

In our culture, there is pressure to keep doing, doing, doing. But remember, our mission is to live a full life, not a busy one. Fullness means you are balancing your need to do and your need to be, because both are essential for your overall health and well-being. The RTZ can be a challenging zone to protect. Sometimes, without even thinking about it, you may treat your fill time as if it is optional, believing that your self-care is something you do only if and when you have the time. You need to fight against this tendency.

One of the best ways to make fill time a part of your routine is to treat these times as if they are appointments on your weekly schedule. For example, when you schedule your semiannual teeth cleaning at the dentist, the appointment time is noted on your calendar. There is a block of time you have purposefully assigned to that commitment. You may even be sent a reminder about the appointment, and there's a good chance you might also get charged a fee if you don't show up for your scheduled time. The appointment is a priority, and there is a consequence if you don't keep it.

Make a promise to yourself to treat your fill time the same way you would treat any other obligation. You want to be healthy, and you need to value taking care of yourself. You must stop thinking of your fill time as optional; instead, consider it a requirement. View your fill time activities in your RTZ in the same way that you view scheduled appointments on your calendar—mandatory and immovable.

When I reflect back on my life, I realize that the seasons I am most dedicated to morning quiet times (part of my RTZ) are when I intentionally schedule them on my calendar. By first committing on paper and on purpose to my RTZ, I am always more motivated to follow through. My calendar helps to hold me accountable (rather than pushing the snooze button again and again!). And the most beautiful part? On those days, my pace of life feels better. After spending some time with God, allowing him to speak to me, I am more than ready to press on because he has helped to fill and equip me.

In a recent conversation with a friend, I asked her how she refills her cup. She told me, "I have my self-care down!" I loved hearing this. She knows that she needs to protect her time for self-care. If she wants to mother her children, manage her home, and be there for her clients, her RTZ must remain a top priority in order for her to be healthy and productive.

Of course, there will be times when you need to go with the flow, but don't get in the habit of moving your fill time further and further down your to-do list. When asked to spend some of your fill time on a task that falls into another time zone, try responding with "I'm sorry, I'm already booked at that time" or "That won't work for me, I already have an appointment." The times set aside for your RTZ should be considered just as valuable as the other appointments on your calendar. This is the time in your schedule when you find a parking space, pull your car in, and stay put.

Learn to echo my friend's words. I want you to get to a place where you can say, "I have my self-care down!"

Following are a few questions to consider when evaluating your RTZ guardrails:

- ▶ What appointments do you need to schedule on your calendar for self-care?

- ▶ What are the common challenges that prevent you from fulfilling your commitment to your RTZ?

- ▶ Are there some boundaries you could put in place to help better protect your fill time?

## Take the Wheel!

As you did for your GTZ and YTZ, you'll now add only your RTZ blocks of time to your schedule for a one-week test drive. Use seven days to evaluate how you are scheduling and protecting your time for self-care.

The number of hours you schedule daily and weekly for your RTZ will vary and be determined by how much time you need to fully experience a recharge. However, this time zone does not fall under my favorite saying, "Less is more." When it comes to your RTZ hours, *more is more*.

Ideally, it is beneficial to have at least one RTZ block of time scheduled every day of the week and, at a minimum, for thirty minutes a day. These thirty minutes may be broken into smaller increments. You may schedule RTZ activities in short blocks of time, such as ten to fifteen minutes sprinkled throughout your day, or long blocks of time, anywhere from one to eight hours. Within your smaller pockets of scheduled fill time, you might flip through a magazine, take a bath, or enjoy a power nap. When you have more time allocated for your RTZ, you might plan a golfing date with your spouse or an entire day shopping with friends.

Mark your RTZ hours and activities on either your personal calendar or the weekly schedule that follows. Per your productivity chart (chap. 3), first fill in the times in the left-hand column at which you circled one star. These are your RTZ hours, your least-productive times of the day. Then, referring to the red light box, distribute the activities you listed into the RTZ time blocks for each day of the week. Remember, this week you are working on adding only the RTZ times to your schedule. You may wear your other hats at times but choose to concentrate specifically on what you are doing for *you* this week!

After incorporating your RTZ times and activities for one week, evaluate your results. Compare and contrast whether what you planned and scheduled was what was realized as you reflect on the following questions:

- ▸ Were you able to protect your RTZ hours?

- ▸ How did you experience restoration in your RTZ?

- ▸ Were there too few (or too many) hours dedicated to your fill time?

## Weekly Schedule: RTZ

| Time | Sunday | Monday | Tuesday | Wednesday | Thursday | Friday | Saturday |
|------|--------|--------|---------|-----------|----------|--------|----------|
|      |        |        |         |           |          |        |          |
|      |        |        |         |           |          |        |          |
|      |        |        |         |           |          |        |          |
|      |        |        |         |           |          |        |          |
|      |        |        |         |           |          |        |          |
|      |        |        |         |           |          |        |          |
|      |        |        |         |           |          |        |          |
|      |        |        |         |           |          |        |          |
|      |        |        |         |           |          |        |          |
|      |        |        |         |           |          |        |          |
|      |        |        |         |           |          |        |          |
|      |        |        |         |           |          |        |          |

Just as with your GTZ and your YTZ, this was a practice run for how to more intentionally add your RTZ to your schedule. The idea is to help you start thinking about self-care in a new way. Value the time you dedicate to you. Your "me" time, your time for you, is important!

Avoid bonking at all costs. Schedule your required maintenance so you have time to refuel, refresh, relate, relax, rest, and restore. Commit to being a Nurturing Lady who values her fill time just as much as her focus and flex times.

Be an example of how to nurture not only others but also yourself. You are worth it. Return to the well, so the well doesn't run dry for everyone and everything else.

### Tip—Three Ways to Create Time for Self-Care

▶ *Plan*. Look closely at your schedule and see where you already have some margin built into your calendar that could be used for self-care. Then intentionally schedule and commit to some self-care time. Consider it an appointment that is nonnegotiable. Be realistic about how much time you need for self-care, and don't cut corners. Allow yourself the time you need to fully recharge.

▶ *Prepare*. Once you've scheduled your time for self-care, prepare that time for success. For example, do you need to make a standing appointment for a monthly pedicure? Or buy a new journal for your gratitude and prayer time? Or download more podcasts for your walks? Or tuck your kids in bed earlier so you can relax in a nightly bath before bed? Organize the details surrounding your self-care time so you will be fully prepared to be restored when the time comes.

▶ *Protect*. After planning and preparing, create a hedge of protection around your self-care time. During this designated time, unplug from all of your other roles. Use healthy boundaries and communicate well with the people in your life about the time you've committed to self-care. The exact amount of time is going to be up to you. It will be based on what you need. Some weeks you may need more time for self-care than other weeks. Protect your time so you can experience the restoration you need.

> Take back your time—
> RED means stop!

# 7

# Your Design

## Applying Your Strengths

> You cannot be anything you want to be—but you can
> be a lot more of who you already are.
>
> Tom Rath

I am convinced that nothing has humbled me more than being a parent. I say this even more now, as I'm thick in the throes of raising three teenagers. Being a parent to teenagers is a wonderful yet emotional and exhausting season of life.

When my kids were toddlers, I was committed to following a predictable daily routine. Having our meal, play, and nap times planned out made our days flow more smoothly. It seemed that by staying on a schedule, my children were better eaters and nappers. There were, of course, meltdowns, whining sessions, and full-blown fits. However, by staying on what I like to call a *flexi-schedule* that resembled a fairly predictable routine, we had an increased sense of calm in our day to day.

I'm not proud to admit that as a young mother I was incredibly quick to judge other parents when their kids misbehaved, especially when it appeared to me that their children were not on a schedule. If another parent's child was throwing a major temper tantrum or flat-out refusing to obey, I would assume it was due to their lack of routine. When witnessing another mom or dad struggling with their child's behavior, I would find myself thinking, *They need to put their kids on a schedule. Kids thrive on structure. Parents need to be calling the shots.* At the time, my perspective was that of a momma whose first two children were super solid sleepers and not picky eaters.

When Berkley, our third child, was born, I quickly realized I was going to have to be more fluid with her schedule than I had been with my older two. Berkley was joining an already full family and a full schedule! This reality meant I was bringing her with me to soccer practices and nursing her on the sidelines. I was strapping her into her stroller and wheeling her into the elementary school so I could fulfill my volunteer commitments to my older children's classrooms. I was also keeping her up later in the evenings because of school events, midweek church services, or socializing with our friends. Berkley's daily rhythm was not as consistent or organized as it had been for Ainsley and Connor. I'm happy to say that all in all, she went with the flow and naturally settled into her role as our youngest family member. She is hardwired with lots of energy, which helped her to keep up the pace as the fifth member of our team.

One afternoon while tidying up the kitchen and preparing dinner during my cherished afternoon nap time for the children, I got the sense that someone had joined me in the kitchen; in fact, I could feel that someone was standing behind me. I quickly turned around, and there before me was my darling, just-turned-two-year-old Berkley. She had not only decided she was not going to take a nap but had also decided to climb out of her crib and come find me. This was a complete shock! I had never had a child escape from their crib at nap time! Ainsley and Connor had both taken naps until kindergarten.

Obviously, Berkley had a plan of her own, and she had neglected to send me the memo.

After the nap-time escape-artist incident, we not only transitioned Berkley from her crib to a big-girl bed but also came to the painful realization that she no longer needed to nap. No matter my attempts to schedule a nap for her, my sweet girl did not and to this day does not need much sleep.

So yes, I ate some major humble pie after that escapade, and I had to adjust to having a nap-free, energetic two-year-old. I learned to accept, in a fresh new way, that my children are uniquely designed and hardwired and that they each have different energy levels.

When I describe Berkley to someone, I say that she has David's outgoing personality and my high energy level. She is often the last one to fall asleep in our home and the first one to wake. At age nine, she wrote and sang a duet with her friend in front of her entire school. Then, upon completion of the song and completely off script, Berkley asked her principal for a turn with the microphone so she could say a few words. She proceeded to pay tribute to her singing partner and basically replicated a strong Oscar-award-winning acceptance speech.

I love seeing how God has designed and shaped my little girl. When I see her unique personality and high capacity for living life to the fullest, I am excited to think about all the wonderful possibilities in her future. Berkley has been shaped by God to be exactly who she is. I am extremely grateful I get to be her momma. (Even though this momma could have used another year or two of nap time.)

## Personality and Capacity

All of us find ourselves overwhelmed and without enough time on occasion. I believe this is often because we are choosing to do things that don't fit within our unique personalities, capacities, and energies. We are each designed and shaped in beautiful and individual ways, and we need to embrace this gift from God.

This statement by Ann Voskamp is convicting: "Your time is limited—so don't limit your life by wanting someone else's."[1] Being created in a unique way means that your time and your life are personal. It is essential to recognize how you have been shaped and lovingly embrace your specific hardwiring if you want to make the most of your time.

When working as a human resources manager, one of my duties was to plan and execute company parties. For some people, this may sound like a dream job. "I get to go to Costco during my workday and buy food to feed one-hundred-plus people? Fun!"

At the beginning, I thought it sounded fun too. However, after I had a few parties under my belt, I realized that playing the role of party planner is not my cup of tea. I found it challenging to cater to people's individual tastes, and by no means would you ever call me a foodie. While I can easily handle the details, numbers, and administrative pieces, planning and executing large work parties was not a good fit for me.

The good news is that for many people, party planning and executing *are* their strengths. They love everything about throwing parties, and this is why they are the best people for the job!

When living in Portugal, I was asked to be the swim meet director for our daughters' swim team. After giving the decision some careful consideration, I decided that this commitment would be a good use of my time. As the director, I was required to plan and host three home swim meets over the course of the swim season for a variety of international swim teams. It was an administrative job that included many things I naturally like to do, tasks such as organizing, communicating, and scheduling. The only food involved was a lunch for the volunteers, which I promptly delegated to a natural-born hostess. Planning a swim meet requires a lot of preliminary, behind-the-scenes work. Then on the weekend of the event, I had to be there early in the morning for setup to ensure all my planning was being properly executed. When the meets were underway, I could be found happily carrying around a clipboard, acting as the go-to person and problem solver, and loving every minute of it! It was a big responsibility, and I enjoyed the entire process. This job played to my strengths and felt like a natural fit. I felt energized in this role and truly enjoyed the challenge.

In *Strengths Finder 2.0*, author Tom Rath shares:

> Over the past decade, Gallup has surveyed more than 10 million people worldwide on the topic of employee engagement (or how positive and productive people are at work), and only one-third "strongly agree" with the statement: "*At work I have the opportunity to do what I do best every day.*"
>
> And for those who do *not* get to focus on what they do best—their strengths—the costs are staggering. In a recent poll of more than 1,000 people, among those who "strongly disagreed" or "disagreed" with this "what I do best" statement, *not one single person* was emotionally engaged on the job.
>
> In stark contrast, our studies indicate that people who *do* have the opportunity to focus on their strengths every day are *six times as likely to be engaged in their jobs* and more than *three times as likely to report having an excellent quality of life in general*.[2]

Whatever it is you are called to spend your time on, when you are able to utilize your strengths, you are much more likely to feel engaged. Whether personally or professionally, when you play to your strengths, you will be maximizing your efforts and increasing your feelings of accomplishment. You will be able to persevere, experience more success than stress, and best of all your time will feel as though it was time well spent.

There will be occasions when we'll need to stretch ourselves and work on things that may fall outside our comfort zones. However, remember that when it comes to the bigger picture of managing your time well, the more you play to your strengths the better off you will be. When you are able to incorporate your strengths, it will naturally have a direct, positive impact on the results.

Commit to focusing on your personality strengths. When you know *who* you are and *how* you tick, you will be able to make the best choices with your time. You will have increased clarity with what to commit to and you will be more successful at setting up your calendar and utilizing the three time zones.

### Your Personality

Generally speaking, there are four main personality types. You can go into much more depth on the study of personalities, and there are many different methods of determining your personality type, but for the purposes of this book, we are going to keep it simple.

The four personality types I've identified fall under what I refer to as the "shape" styles: arrows, bolts, circles, and diamonds.

Your *shape* is defined by how you tick — what you do or don't do naturally. It is your personality, the way you look at life, and how you interact with others. Think of your shape as your inward and outward responses to life. Within the outline of your shape lay your clear-cut strengths.

*Arrow shapes: the friend who is often in charge, a natural leader.* Arrows are driven, dedicated, competitive, and focused. They are able to accomplish almost everything they set their minds to. Organizing is in their DNA, along with efficiency and problem solving. They are usually more than willing to delegate areas of their life to qualified people who are able to assist them. They have a very traditional and functional way of organizing their spaces and time.

*Bolt shapes: the friend you call whenever you want to have some serious fun.* Bolts are energetic, motivating, future oriented, and optimistic. They are able to inspire others with their enthusiasm and their great communication skills. Their tendency is to have great ideas with a lot of creativity, while sometimes not realizing the details that are involved. They are often artists and have a very adventurous side. They are comfortable with their belongings being around them and have the mentality that more is more!

*Circle shapes: the friend who sympathizes with you and is always supportive.* Circles are relational, loyal, sensitive, and peacemakers. They are able to counsel others and usually reach out to help others. Their lives can sometimes feel a bit overwhelmed because they have a hard time saying the word *no*. When they say yes, they are loyal and will pour their hearts and energy into what they commit to do. Circles prefer their surroundings to be very personable, decorative, and comfortable. Aesthetics are very important to circles.

*Diamond shapes: the friend who is detailed and has excellent follow-through.* Diamonds are precise, analytical, disciplined, and consistent. They are able to keep focused on the facts, listen well, and follow through with excellent quality control, although at times with a little too much seriousness. They are born organized and strongly believe in having a place for everything and everything in its place.

Diamonds are all about the details. The more detail oriented the better. Planning and order are where they thrive!

After reading through the different shape definitions, ask yourself which shape you most identify and resonate with. You will likely have a primary and a secondary shape. You may also see a little bit of yourself in each of the four shapes. Think about how you act and behave the majority of the time and what your default responses and reactions are to life.

| Arrows | Bolts |
|---|---|
| Traditional and functional ways of organizing their spaces and time. | Organic and creative ways of organizing their spaces and time. |
| **Circles** | **Diamonds** |
| Colorful and relaxed ways of organizing their spaces and time. | Detailed and structured ways of organizing their spaces and time. |

In terms of the four shapes, I am a primary diamond and a secondary circle. My brain naturally works in a very detailed manner. I prefer structure, and most of the time I would rather be the listener than the speaker. My circle shape is evidenced by my easygoing personality, my go-with-the-flow attitude, and yes, my people-pleasing tendencies. I have some parts of an arrow in me as I am the firstborn in my family and am happy to lead when asked. The only time you will see any bolt shape come out is likely on the dance floor. Otherwise, I am quite reserved and tend to be more of a private person.

The beautiful part is that we are perfectly created in our own shape. God wants us to operate differently from one another. He designed us this way. We are meant to complement one another. We all have strengths, and we all have weaknesses. We are like puzzle pieces, and our various shapes help us to fit together better.

Now if the foot should say, "Because I am not a hand, I do not belong to the body," it would not for that reason stop being part of the body. And if the ear should say, "Because I am not an eye, I do not belong to the body," it would not for that reason stop being part of the body. If the whole body were an eye, where would the sense of hearing be? If the whole body were an ear, where would the sense of smell be? But in fact God has placed the parts in the body, every one of them, just as he wanted them to be. If they were all one part, where would the body be? As it is, there are many parts, but one body.

The eye cannot say to the hand, "I don't need you!" And the head cannot say to the feet, "I don't need you!" On the contrary, those parts of the body that seem to be weaker are indispensable, and the parts that we think are less honorable we treat with special honor. And the parts that are unpresentable are treated with special modesty, while our presentable parts need no special treatment. But God has put the body together, giving greater honor to the parts that lacked it, so that there should be no division in the body, but that its parts should have equal concern for each other. If one part suffers, every part suffers with it; if one part is honored, every part rejoices with it.

Now you are the body of Christ, and each one of you is a part of it. (1 Cor. 12:15–27)

When we each play to the strengths of our personal shape, we are able to bring out the best in ourselves and each other.

God has designed *you* exactly how he wanted you to be; therefore, claim your style! Knowing your strengths will help you to know how and where to most focus your time. In *Work Simply*, Carson Tate writes, "You cannot outwork your busyness using one-size-fits-all time management solutions. The latest app, prioritization tip, or email management strategy will not work if it is not personalized for you, aligned with the way you think and process information. Instead, it will only create even more frustration, inefficiency, and ineffectiveness."[3]

If you are an arrow, look at your schedule and evaluate which items you can and should be delegating. Play to this strength. Continue to set goals, and remember to make time to relax!

If you are a bolt, try using a timer. A timer can help you to stay on track with your time. Make a point to ask for help when you need it, and keep things you are working on in your visual space.

If you are a circle, a beautiful day planner with a colorful set of stylish pens can help motivate you. Commit to writing down your to-dos, and design a comfortable and calming space for your time of work.

If you are a diamond, don't overschedule your schedule. As a taskmaster by nature, be very intentional about giving yourself enough margin between your various appointments and activities. Also, strive to think more outside the box, adapting when necessary.

Acknowledging both your strengths and your weaknesses will improve your ability to strike a harmonious balance when scheduling your time zones. For example:

▶ As an arrow, you may be prone to forgetting to schedule your foundational RTZ hours. Remember to be good to yourself, making time for your self-care. Having fun is just as important as getting work done. And when you safeguard your RTZ hours, you will experience even more productivity.

▶ As a bolt, you may need to put more boundaries in place when you work in your GTZ. Distractions are fun, but when working in your GTZ, you need to stay focused. Your desk may look like a tornado hit it most of the time, but that is OK because this works for you.

▶ As a circle, you might be saying yes to more commitments than you have time for, which means that when you are working in your YTZ you are trying to do too many things at the same time. Give yourself permission to say no! You do not have to be all things to all people. If you are the one always saying yes, you may be limiting others from being able to step up to the plate.

▶ As a diamond, you might be scheduling too many hours in your GTZ, which is negatively impacting your ability to be present in your relationships or other life activities. Allow yourself time to just be! There will always be more to do. Balance out your need to do with your need to be. Learn to be even more flexible, especially when working in your YTZ. It's OK to not always finish each and every task you start. Remember, there is always tomorrow.

Recognizing your natural tendencies can help you to weed out those things that negatively impact your ability to manage your time. Playing to your strengths and remaining faithful to color within the lines of your shape will help you to make the most of your time in each of your zones.

### *Your Capacity*

After identifying your personality shape, it is also helpful to consider whether you are wired more as an introvert or an extrovert and how this affects your capacity and energy levels in relation to your time.

Understanding whether you are extroverted or introverted will help you to know what types of activities fill you or drain you and whether you focus better working in a group or independently. You will have a new perspective on why you are the way you are and why certain events or obligations energize you or tire you out.

Wikipedia defines *extroversion* and *introversion* in this way:

> Extraversion is the state of primarily obtaining gratification from outside oneself. Extraverts tend to enjoy human interactions and to be enthusiastic, talkative, assertive, and gregarious. Extraverts are energized and thrive off being around other people. They take pleasure in activities that involve large social gatherings, such as parties, community activities, public demonstrations, and business or political groups. They also tend to work well in groups. An extraverted person is likely to enjoy time spent with people and find less reward in time spent alone. They tend to be energized when around other people, and they are more prone to boredom when they are by themselves.
>
> Introversion is the state of being predominantly interested in one's own mental self. Introverts are typically perceived as more reserved or reflective. Some popular psychologists have characterized introverts as people whose energy tends to expand through reflection and dwindle during interaction. . . . Introverts often take pleasure in solitary activities such as reading, writing, using computers, hiking or fishing. . . . An introvert is likely to enjoy time spent alone and find less reward in time spent with large groups of people, though they may enjoy interactions with close friends.[4]

Berkley, if you haven't guessed by now, is a bolt and extroverted. She doesn't need as much time to recharge as I do. I am an introvert; I crave my alone time. I typically get drained after being in large groups and most definitely prefer smaller gatherings and time spent one-on-one.

However, like Berkley, I also have a high energy level. So, for me to reset and keep my energy levels where they naturally want to be, I must intentionally plan and schedule enough time to be by myself. On the flip side, because I have a high capacity, I also have a strong need to have many items on my to-do list. If my day is underscheduled or lacks routine, it is tougher for me to feel motivated. I do better when I have some pressure on my time. When there are deadlines and bookends in place, I am more driven. The feeling of just enough pressure helps me to stay on task and be more productive.

In my time zones, I prefer to work quietly and independently, especially in my GTZ. When working in my YTZ, I am careful when possible to not schedule more than three to four hours at one time. This is the time zone that can drain me the most if it goes on for more than four hours. And, when I consider which RTZ activity to schedule, I almost always choose something I can do solo.

You can be any shape and be either introverted or extroverted. You may also find that you are extroverted in some circumstances and introverted in other circumstances. You may have high energy levels in certain situations and low energy levels in other situations. Commonly, arrows and bolts are more extroverted, and circles and diamonds are more introverted, but there are no strict rules. Our God is a creative God! Remember that these labels are not either-or but are set on a continuum. Don't let the labels limit you! Allow them to act as guides.

I may be an introvert, but I love getting up on stage and teaching a fitness class to a room full of people. I thrive in this environment because I like the opportunity to put on my extroverted hat every once in a while. However, I find that after teaching for an hour, I usually need a good refill. I need some time in my RTZ simply because being extroverted isn't my natural bent.

Don't limit yourself or use your personality or capacity as a roadblock. You can challenge yourself to grow in some of your weaker areas, but realize you are hardwired to be exactly who you are. Understanding your personality and capacity and how they work together will help guide you in scheduling your time and help you to know how best to prioritize your priorities. Your choices make up your time; therefore, it is critical to make good choices.

Now when I'm asked to plan a party or host a large event, I think twice about it and usually say no, because I'm working on my people-pleasing tendency and I know this role isn't the best fit for me. Someone who is a primary arrow and a secondary circle is probably much better suited. However, if I'm asked to volunteer for something solely administrative, I confidently raise my hand high.

Play to your strengths—your productivity and your peace depend on it. Your strengths are what allow you to be the beautiful person God designed you to be. Let your strengths help you shine!

## Start, Stop, Continue

One exercise I learned in a training session was called Start, Stop, Continue. It is designed to be used by two coworkers to help with communication and team building. In the training, we each had to share with another person one thing we would like them to start doing, one thing to stop doing, and one thing to continue doing. It was challenging to be so direct and honest with feedback. However, this approach to confronting issues helped to foster important conversations and resolve conflicts.

As a family, we do this activity from time to time, and I love hearing from everyone. I also like being able to share feedback with them—for example, "I would like for you to start loading your dishes."

When it comes to scheduling and your time, I want you to take into consideration your personality and capacity and work through this exercise on your own. Consider what you need to start doing, stop doing, and continue doing when it comes to your time. Using what you have learned about your current season, your schedule snapshot, your productivity, the time zones, and your design, highlight what is working and what could be working better for you when it comes to time management. Consider the following questions:

- ▶ What do you need to be careful to avoid when planning and scheduling?

- ▶ Which zone is the least natural for you to safeguard?

- ▶ When do you feel the most overwhelmed within your day or week and why?

- ▶ How do you feel at the end of most days?

- ▶ What priorities do you have the hardest time protecting and why?

I'll go first. Here is an example.

Start: scheduling more RTZ on my weekly schedule
(goal = one hour a day)
Stop: trying to do more than two or three tasks at one
time in my YTZ
Continue: writing down my weekly to-do list

Now it's your turn.

Start:
Stop:
Continue:

This is an exercise you can repeat again and again. It works as a great tool to help fine-tune how you organize your time.

You can take this a step further and complete the exercise with a spouse or a friend, asking them what they think you need to start, stop, and continue doing. When you ask someone else to provide you with feedback, you will most certainly learn new things about yourself. Ask specifically in regard to how you are spending your time and what you are choosing to commit to.

What other people share with us can help open our eyes to those things we haven't been able to notice for ourselves. David is a great sounding board for me. He knows my design and that I get excited about any and every opportunity that comes my way. My high energy level has been known to cloud my reality, but he is good at helping me to look at things from a big-picture perspective. I make a point to run things by him and seek his feedback. David needs more downtime than I do, and he has a different capacity than me. However, I value his input, because I know he always has my best interests at heart.

Don't fall into the trap of wondering how other people get so much done. (They are probably delegating more than you.) Or how that person seems to have everything together. (They don't!) Or why you are not getting anything accomplished in your particular season of life. (You are, and you have different seasons ahead of you.) Or why you are wired the way you are and wishing you were wired differently. (Stop this, you are perfect!)

Ladies, I encourage you to stay in your own lane of life. God wants you to be good at what you are good at! You are unique and therefore your time is personal.

For me, this means I'm not heading to Costco to buy food for a large work party. Nor am I going to lie down and take a nap; I have too much energy. Instead, I'm rewriting my to-do list because I'm a detailed diamond. And because I'm also shaped as a comfy circle, I'm heading out to shop for more pillows for our comfy couch. I firmly believe that one can never have too many pillows.

### Tip—Stay in Your Lane

▶ Keep your eyes on the horizon, looking ahead to where you intend to go.

▶ Keep your hands open, willing to do what you are called to do.

▶ Keep your heart humble, using your gifts to bless others.

> Take back your time—
> color within the lines
> of your shape!

# 8

# Your Calendar

## Merging Your Time Zones

What may be done at any time will be done at no time.

Scottish proverb

One of my favorite family vacations is a visit to a Disney theme park. There is something magical about stepping into a fairy-tale kingdom that encourages me to be a kid again. Between grabbing fast passes, watching performers, and eating ice cream, I marvel at how a theme park of that size is able to run so smoothly day in and day out. I wonder how they are able to organize and schedule their enormous staff and run such a tight operation. From my point of view, it seems as though the staff at Disney is running a three-ring (or more) circus, and things are going off without a hitch.

Disneyland resort, located in California, has between twenty-three thousand and twenty-six thousand employees.[1]

That is a lot of people to schedule in order to adequately staff the rides, restaurants, shows, and so on. After experiencing firsthand the high standards Disney has for their service and cleanliness and how no detail goes unnoticed, it appears to me that they have their priorities and scheduling down to a science.

I realize they rely on computer programs, detailed spreadsheets, and past data to help with the logistics, but no matter how you slice it, this is a scheduling puzzle with thousands and thousands of pieces! Impeccable planning is what allows Disney to open their doors for business. Their employees are precisely scheduled around the clock, making it possible for Disney to operate 365 days a year without interruption.

The managers at Disney know they have a tight ship to run. They know that time matters. They know they must schedule their employees intentionally and efficiently or the park will suffer in decreased sales. Can you imagine if Disney's employees were told to come to work only when they wanted to or when they felt like it? Or if their supervisors said they could choose to work wherever they wanted when they did decide to show up for work? This would not provide a good experience for Disney's guests nor be an effective way to schedule or manage their employees.

Of course, businesses must schedule their time; after all, they are businesses. And yes, I should probably learn to relax a bit more while visiting a theme park! However, I find it interesting that while we can fully embrace a business, school, or organization having a timetable and fixed calendar, we don't always apply this same form of planning and scheduling to our own lives and personal calendars.

Instead, we often *hope* to get things done rather than *plan* to get things done. But hope is not a strategy: *anytime* is a dangerous way to approach time management. You don't want to leave things to chance. You want to ensure that you schedule what needs to be scheduled and plan what needs to be planned.

## Planning

First things first. You need to keep a calendar. Maintaining a calendar is vital if you want to organize your time and make your time work for you. Having a place to type or write everything down is essential to good time management. If you haven't developed this habit, make a commitment to do so.

Your calendar should take whatever form works best for you. It may be a digital calendar, wall calendar, or day planner. Anything goes! If you are not sure what type you prefer, take some time to explore different options and see which one sticks. Most importantly, you want to learn which method you are able to keep most organized. If you choose a digital calendar, look at Cozi, Apple, Microsoft, or Google. If you prefer a wall calendar or day planner, there is every kind of style available.

My suggestion is to keep *only one calendar*. You should not have a desk calendar at work for work appointments and deadlines, a calendar app on your phone for your kids' activities, and a wall calendar at home for family birthdays and anniversaries. What usually happens when you have multiple calendars is that you will miss something, because an item listed on one calendar is not listed on another and vice versa. Having multiple calendars can easily result in double booking or forgetting about an appointment altogether. You may elect to have different calendars set up within one calendar system. For example, I use a digital Google calendar and have different calendars set up within it: one for home maintenance, one for birthdays, one for work, and so on. This works well because I can still see all my appointments and events on one screen on one application.

This should be your goal with your calendar system— everything in one place. Organizing a calendar system will be the foundation of your planning and scheduling efforts.

As I shared previously, you will have different types of days. On some days, everything clicks along; on others, you may feel like you are taking two steps forward and one step back. You will have days that go differently than you plan. But none of this means you shouldn't plan. It just means you need to remain adaptable, especially when plans go awry.

When David and I began to prepare for our move overseas, he mentioned that we should have a planning meeting. I agreed and we scheduled a time to discuss and go over things. He informed me that he would be bringing home his calendar so we could go over all the logistics. This comment from him surprised me because I never knew him to keep a calendar. He is more of a "fly by the seat of his pants" kind of a guy.

The night of our meeting, I was seated at the kitchen table with my color-coded Google calendar displayed on my laptop when David walked in. Tucked under his arm was a supersized desk calendar from his office. If memory serves me right, the front page was not even turned to the current month. He spread his large calendar down on the table, taking up almost the entire surface, and I couldn't help but laugh! (He has since switched to using a digital Google calendar, which is much more convenient, not to mention easier to carry around.)

Find your preferred calendar system and commit to using it. Remember that when it comes to planning, you want to strike a harmony between hyperscheduling (where everything is planned down to the minute) and haphazard scheduling (where you don't plan a single thing). Staying somewhere between these two extremes and utilizing the three time zones is how you will experience harmony.

## Reflecting and Listening

Disney schedules their staff efficiently because they continually look in their rearview mirror at the past numbers of attendees and ticket sales. Evaluating this data helps them know how to best prepare for the future.

We too can look in our rearview mirrors and see where our scheduling has worked well for us in the past. However, as we look ahead to the future, we have something even more powerful than computer statistics to help us with our planning. We have God's guidance and wisdom. Because God is above and outside the sphere of time, he is a powerful source for us to lean into and seek direction from. "But do not forget this one thing, dear friends: With the Lord a day is like a thousand years, and a thousand years are like a day" (2 Pet. 3:8).

Listening to God will help you discern how and where to spend your time. He cares about every single detail of your life, including your schedule. But to hear what God wants you to do with your time, it is vital that you spend time listening to him. I love what Micah Maddox shared in her book, *Anchored In*:

> We rush around doing what we think is important, and we miss the words that God is trying to speak into our hearts. We want to hear Him, but life simply gets in the way, and we miss Him. Sometimes we start out with big, bold plans of doing something amazing for God only to get swept up in the details, the stress of the daily grind, and the distractions of the to-do list that is seemingly required to get the job done. Oh, how foolish we can be when it comes to what is important. We often choose the current over the eternal. And when we do, often we see later how our choice to focus on what felt crucial was really a distraction from what God was trying to draw us to—Himself.[2]

Listening to God will help you know what to most focus on. He will guide you and assist you in finding the middle ground in your planning and scheduling—what I like to think of as the sweet spot. There are many definitions of *sweet spot*, but I like this one: "The sweet spot is a place where a combination of factors results in a maximum response for a given amount of effort."[3]

Whether professionally or personally, the sweet spot experience is when you hit a tennis ball, golf ball, or baseball just right. It feels good, it feels like you nailed it, like your plans were perfect. The sweet spot in time management is when and where you find serenity and feel at peace. The sweet spot is when you are planning and scheduling in a way that honors God, yourself, and other people.

I want us to live lives with less panic and more peace, more sweetness, more right.

There are areas in my life when I do not hit the ball in the sweet spot. This happens when I take my eyes off the ball (the ball of objectivity) or when I'm not listening to God and his perfect plan for my life. God's guidance helps us to experience the sweetness of the spot. The sweet spot is that wonderful space between having and giving, passivity and controlling, organizing and hoarding, stressing and relaxing, talking and listening, leading and following, acting and watching, spending and saving, and doing and being.

I continue to search out the sweet spot, the spot where I am not overly rigid nor overly relaxed. I want to be more in the middle, more in the sweet spot.

The most significant thing you can do to positively impact your time management and find the sweet spot is to lean into God and his direction for your time. He has given you the Holy Spirit to help you through each hour of your life. Press into his guidance and his still, small voice. When you do, you will experience more peace, more harmony, and more of the sweet spot surrounding how you organize and spend your time.

## Scheduling

After some practice with implementing the time zones, you should have a new perspective of what the zones mean for you and how best to use them within your weekly schedule. My hope is that as you added each time zone, you began to recognize which time zone you were in as you moved through your day.

For example, I recently treated myself to a pedicure, and as I settled into the massage chair and opened my book, I found myself thinking, *I'm in my RTZ.* I was taking an hour for myself, for self-care, and it was glorious. I was able to refill because I took the time necessary to slow down and stop. The other evening while in my YTZ, I juggled cleaning up the kitchen, making a batch of Almond Roca (a traditional dessert we make every Christmas), and instructing my kids to complete their chores. My time was being flexed between separate but complementary tasks. As I type these words, I am focused. I am actively working in my GTZ. My email inbox is shut down, my phone ringer is turned off, and I am the only one at home. Things are quiet, which allows me to focus and get my work done.

Now you are going to shift gears, from planning, reflecting, and listening to scheduling—listing what you need to do and when you will do it. You are going to take the three distinct time zones and organize them as a trio, as the Three Amigos, in your weekly schedule. This is where you take everything you have learned and put it all together. Now is the time to take back your time!

Begin by considering the picture of your weekly schedule. Remember to seek fullness, schedule margin, and stay adaptable. Keep in mind that you may need to shift between two or even three time zones. Consider revisiting your time log (chap. 2) and productivity chart (chap. 3). There is some valuable information you can take away from those exercises that can be applied when scheduling the three zones.

Following are a few examples of how to schedule the three time zones. Respecting your design (personality and capacity), determine a good option for you. And feel free to create your own way of organizing the time zones. Implementing and then merging the time zones will require some trial and error. However, once it becomes a habit, it will be easier and easier to employ and to produce maximum results!

### Weekly View

If you tend to have a more consistent weekly routine, then a big-picture view of your schedule is a good way to visualize where your time zones will fall. To create a weekly view, use a one-week sample of your schedule and time block the three zones throughout your week. (You can download a free printable of a weekly schedule at www.morganizewithme.com/shop.)

The weekly view is an hour by hour and time zone by time zone master schedule. This view is like when your GPS provides you with the line between your start and finish points. You don't see the play-by-play but you know the overall map. A big-picture weekly schedule is something you can pin on a bulletin board, tape to your bathroom mirror, or hang on the refrigerator. This will be your guide when you organize your calendar and commitments. Unlike a weekly calendar, this weekly time zone schedule does not need to include specific appointments and activities. It will highlight only the blocks of time and the different time zones you feel you can allocate to each. It will be used as a reference and will remind you when to be in each time zone. It is a proactive and deliberate approach that will also remain flexible for whatever comes your way. It is also OK to have some empty blocks. This is where you leave room for margin.

A big-picture view of your weekly schedule is often best if you have more of a set or fixed schedule. For example, if you work part-time Monday through Friday, you could mark these hours as either GTZ, YTZ, or a combination of the two, depending on your type of work. If you stay home to care for your young children, you could note your morning times as YTZ because you are flexing between childcare and home care. Then your afternoon times could be listed as GTZ, the precious and hopefully productive times when your children are napping. Or, maybe even better, these afternoon hours could be your RTZ hours when you too can get some rest!

Following is an example of a weekly schedule with time zones assigned to each specific hour. This option may work well if you are a primary bolt or circle as it serves as a visual reminder.

### Daily View

If you prefer to plan each day on an individual basis, then a daily view would be a better choice. A small-picture view means that each day you highlight the three time zones on your calendar. This option is a good fit if your week tends to vary and no two days look the same. The daily view allows you to take specific scheduling steps daily.

When scheduling your day to day, you don't necessarily need to assign time zones to every single hour of every single day. And make sure to allow some natural blending and shifting between the zones. You do not want to schedule every sixty minutes of your day and then feel overwhelmed when life happens.

If you prefer more detail and less vision—I'm speaking to the arrows and the diamonds out there—you may want to consider incorporating a daily view of the three time zones into your calendar. This view is similar to selecting the turn-by-turn directions on your GPS. These directions assist you in navigating each and every turn that comes your way.

### Task View

If you work best from the viewpoint of your tasks or your to-do list (which I will cover in more detail in the next section), you may find that the best way for you to merge your three time zones is to schedule the zones from the perspective of your tasks. This could look like assigning a specific color to each of your to-do tasks—green, yellow, or red. Then, as you refer to your to-do list throughout

## Weekly Schedule

| Time | Sunday | Monday | Tuesday | Wednesday | Thursday | Friday | Saturday |
|------|--------|--------|---------|-----------|----------|--------|----------|
| 6:00 a.m. | Red | Yellow | Red | Yellow | Red | Yellow | Red |
| 7:00 a.m. | Red | Yellow | Red | Yellow | Red | Yellow | Red |
| 8:00 a.m. | Red | Green | Yellow | Green | Yellow | Green | Green |
| 9:00 a.m. | Yellow | Green | Yellow | Green | Yellow | Green | Green |
| 10:00 a.m. | Yellow | Green | Yellow | Green | Yellow | Green | Yellow |
| 11:00 a.m. | Yellow | Green | Yellow | Green | Yellow | Green | Yellow |
| 12:00 p.m. | Yellow | Yellow | Yellow | Yellow | Yellow | Yellow | Yellow |
| 1:00 p.m. | Yellow | Yellow | Green | Yellow | Green | Yellow | Yellow |
| 2:00 p.m. | Yellow | Yellow | Green | Yellow | Green | Yellow | Yellow |
| 3:00 p.m. | Yellow | Yellow | Green | Yellow | Green | Yellow | Yellow |
| 4:00 p.m. | Yellow | Green | Yellow | Green | Yellow | Green | Yellow |
| 5:00 p.m. | Yellow | Yellow | Yellow | Yellow | Yellow | Yellow | Yellow |
| 6:00 p.m. | Yellow | Yellow | Yellow | Yellow | Yellow | Yellow | Red |
| 7:00 p.m. | Red | Yellow | Yellow | Yellow | Yellow | Yellow | Red |
| 8:00 p.m. | Red | Red | Red | Red | Red | Red | Red |
| 9:00 p.m. | Red | Red | Red | Red | Red | Red | Red |

the week, you would let the colors assigned to each task determine the best time for you to work on each to-do item.

For example, if getting a haircut is on your to-do list, this will naturally fall into the hours in your RTZ. If you've listed errands, these could match up to hours in your YTZ. If you have a scheduled conference call, this would be assigned to your GTZ. The task view is where you intentionally plan out your to-do items and assign them to the appropriate time zone on your calendar. It's taking on a mindset of intentionality and can be very helpful in identifying when to do what task.

If you already have a preferred calendar system, you can begin to implement the three zones into your schedule. If you are still working to narrow down your preferred calendar, you may implement this piece later. No rush!

Here are some personal examples of how I schedule the three time zones on my calendar. For self-care, I list attending my weekly yoga class on Friday as two hours in my RTZ. The two hours I block off for my fill time include my drive and transition time. I note my RTZ activities with an (R). If I was using a paper calendar, I might draw a heart next to my RTZ activities. The symbol of a heart represents taking care of my health. Depending on which form of calendar or list you use, consider using a color code or a symbol that speaks to you.

On weekdays, the hours between 3:00 p.m. and 7:00 p.m. are my YTZ time, because this is when my kids are home from school. This is when I shift gears and transition into mom mode. This is when I drive kids around, make dinner, and tidy up the house. Marking these hours with a (Y) on my calendar reminds me not to schedule any focused tasks during these hours. I also tend to hit a lull in the afternoon, so these hours work well for me to bounce between smaller, less focused to-do tasks. Intentionally add your YTZ blocks of time to your calendar and use a symbol or a color to differentiate this time zone. I like the idea of using a circle shape as I often feel like I am walking in circles and not getting as much done as I would like.

When noting my GTZ hours on my schedule, I start by looking for those pockets of time when I can best concentrate. With an adaptable work schedule, I am usually able to easily schedule client sessions or writing hours around other commitments. If my kids are off school on a Monday, I don't schedule hours to my GTZ for that day. Looking over the rest of the week, I block my GTZ hours with a (G) in appropriate time slots. If you are using a paper calendar, an arrow or a check mark would make for a great reminder for your GTZ. This is the zone when you will be checking boxes and moving things forward!

Scheduling and merging the three time zones will help you to accomplish more of what you need to get done. The three zones will equip and encourage you to be more intentional with your time and will increase your ability to focus, flex, or fill, depending on the zone. When you assign the three time zones, you will be providing a better map for your schedule. You will be eliminating the "anytime" syndrome.

As you settle into your daily "commute" of work and tasks, what is most important is that you keep an intentional mindset. When you set about to complete a task, ask yourself if you are working on the task at the right time. Are you in a complementary time zone? Keeping this at the forefront of your mind will do wonders for your productivity. Don't stress about hyperscheduling the time zones. Find what works for you and then stick with it as best you can. The zones should help to keep you in the zone! Your schedule will be a tool to assist you in all that God is calling you to do—whether you choose a weekly view, daily view, task view, or your own view.

## Keeping Lists

### To-Do List

Are you the type of person who keeps a detailed to-do list? Do you add items that you have already completed to your list, just so you can check them off? If so, you most definitely understand the benefit and sense of accomplishment related to having a to-do list.

As with a calendar, a to-do list is one of the most helpful tools for managing your time. A to-do list gives you something to refer to when you are not sure what to work on next, and it provides you with a plan for your time.

If I don't write down a to-do item, whether it's buying three dozen bagels for a Saturday swim meet, purchasing a gift for an upcoming birthday party, or scheduling an oil change for our car, I will most likely forget. If I don't list it, there is no guarantee I will remember to do it.

To-do lists are important because they help us direct our time. When I go grocery shopping with a list, I do a better job of purchasing what we need. Without a list, I lose my focal point. I get drawn into the latest sale or sample and as a result will often bring home things we don't need and forget things we really do need.

Like with your calendar choice, you want to find a method of keeping a to-do list that works for you. Ideally, you want something you can carry with you and refer to easily.

Interestingly, I cannot make a digital to-do list work, despite the fact that I love using a digital calendar. And believe me, I have tried! What does work for me is a small paper notebook or journal. Having something small enough to toss into my purse and carry with me allows me the immediate satisfaction of checking off items from my list as I complete them.

I organize my to-do list on a weekly basis and use a modified bullet-journaling system. A bullet journal is a style of note-taking or journaling that uses bullet points. It's a combination of a planner, diary, and to-do list. I use it specifically as a way to keep all of my lists in one place. What I like about it is that I can personalize it to suit my own style. I use different symbols to notate the status of items on my to-do list as "done," "in progress," or "move forward to the next week." First, I list each to-do item in bullet form. Then I insert a square box next to each item. In each box, I enter a check mark when a task is completed, a dot for a task in progress, and a dash for any task that needs to be moved to the next week. I keep a weekly, running to-do list on a single page (broken down into four categories: home, work, dinner, errands), and each week I prepare a new to-do list. And yes, because life is always in a state of flux, I usually have to move some (or many) items from one week to the next!

If it is helpful for you to have separate to-do lists, go forth and conquer; just work to keep them organized and in one place. Make it a habit to regularly look at your to-do list; daily is a good rule of thumb. Knowing what you need to do will help you to be most effective when scheduling your week. As with your choice of a calendar, try different ways of documenting your to-do list. Once you find a method that works best for you, stick with it. A good to-do list will help you to get more done!

### Done List

Under my purpose of managing and maintaining our home, I can tend to feel as though I'm not getting anything done. I can't tell you how many times I've wiped down a counter, vacuumed a floor, or scrubbed a sink, only to return to it five minutes later to find a fresh mess! Nevertheless, I do not want to be a mom who is vacuuming up behind her kids' footprints, nor do I want to be a wife who limits her husband to sitting only on one couch. (These are not things I have ever done, but I have heard of them being done!) *We can't control things in our lives from becoming undone, but we can control what we get done.*

Another great time-management tool is to create a "done" list each day. This is where you list what you actually accomplish each day. When I do this, I break my day into three parts: morning, afternoon, and evening. Then as I go about my day, I jot down the different things I have completed. Following is an example of a done list for a day in my life:

| Morning (6 a.m.–12 p.m.) | Afternoon (12–6 p.m.) | Evening (6–10 p.m.) |
|---|---|---|
| Quiet time | Went to hair appt. | Made dinner |
| Unloaded DW & tidied | Ran errands | Helped with homework |
| Showered & dressed | Walked dog | Cleaned kitchen |
| Scheduled dentist appts. | Carpooled | Folded & put away laundry |
| Dropped off at school | Worked—emails | Read |
| Worked (9–12)—client | Cleaned great room | |

Writing down what you get done each day can be very satisfying. It allows you to see all that you truly accomplished! You may write down each task or list just the main categories. Personalize your done list so it works for you. The main objective is to show you what you have completed throughout the day. When I feel as though I have done very little over the course of a day, I can look back at my done list and see that I really did accomplish some things. It's a great feeling!

When your done list indicates that you mailed a package, attended a meeting, and returned a phone call, it feels good! You have a visual for how your time was spent in a productive way. It is a very simple tool that can help you to maximize your time. Knowing that you can list a completed task on your done list will motivate you to tackle another item on your to-do list. A done list can improve your aim and show you where your time and efforts are being spent. It can feel like a pat on the back at the end of a long day. I recommend listing each activity, no matter which zone it's in, on your done list. A restorative massage is just as important as finishing a critical work assignment. They are both helpful in fulfilling your purposes.

Practice writing a done list and see how it impacts your ability to organize your time. Continue keeping a done list only if it helps to inspire and motivate you. I don't want it to become one more thing you have to do, especially if it is not beneficial. But if you find it helpful, then by all means, keep doing it.

Whether on paper or on-screen, your priorities need to be organized in a way that works well for you. Planning (using a calendar), reflecting (looking in your rearview mirror), listening (discerning God's direction), scheduling (creating a road map), and keeping lists (writing your to-do lists and done lists) require dedication and discipline. But I guarantee that when you do these things, you will yield much fruit from your labor and experience less hustle and more harmony. Listening to God and having a map for your time will guarantee you are heading in the right direction and spending your time intentionally.

## Tip—Create a Family Weekly Calendar

If you asked my kids if I do a good job of communicating our family commitments to them, all three would loudly respond, "*No!*" Many times I have gotten in trouble for not mentioning we were having people over for dinner (in an hour) or that we all had to attend an event together (and please wear something nice).

A tool that has helped to alleviate this common complaint is a weekly calendar drawn on a chalkboard that lists the highlights for each day, Sunday through Saturday. For example, on Sunday I write "church" and "lunch out as a family." On Tuesday I jot down a 5:00 p.m. soccer practice for Berkley. On Friday I note that we are having the Smiths over for dinner at 6:00 p.m. This schedule takes just a few minutes each week to complete and provides a visual reminder for everyone of shared commitments.

Ask for feedback from your family members about how the family schedule is being communicated. This will tell you if what you are doing is working for everyone. As a family, the more you increase communication about shared commitments, the more you will decrease confusion and potential conflicts.

> Take back your time—
> plan, reflect, listen, schedule,
> and list!

# 9

# Your Goals

## Signaling Your Intention

A year from now you may wish you had started today.

Karen Lamb

till hotel bound and bored, I had tears in my eyes as my heart poured out these words.

I sit on a path along the Portugal coastline. The water is gorgeous and the sun shines with intensity. While walking down to where I now rest, I came to the realization that today marks 21 days of being in Portugal. I have always heard that it takes 21 days to create a new habit. Maybe so. But I don't like my new habit. In fact, deep down I didn't want a new habit. I liked my old habits just fine, my life, my family, my friends, my work, my homey home, frankly there wasn't much I didn't like. Life — not to sound cheesy — was good. I considered it to be a blessed life.

But I did the thing that is so hard to do. I trusted God.

I told Him, that if He opened the door to an overseas transfer, I would walk through it. I wanted to support my man and the Man upstairs. Wow, support, when it involves compromise, is really, really hard. Like the kind of hard where I want to curl up in a ball. A part of me didn't really think that God would put me through this kind of a test. I wanted to believe that the test would be having faith, not necessarily having to follow through. I wasn't scared of a new experience, I just didn't want to let go of my life experience that I knew and loved.

So here I am. Three weeks in Portugal. Wondering why? My life has turned upside down, and not in the way I wanted it to. I don't know what God has in store for me here. I am sad. I am bored. I am frustrated. If I was already living in our house here would that make it better? If I had my car would that help? I am not even sure if these things would make a difference. I think maybe, just maybe, that God moved me to a place over 5000 miles away, from everything I knew and loved, to increase my dependence on Him. Change is hard.

I shared these heartfelt words in a blog post I titled, "Old Habits Die Hard." I realized during this time of self-reflection that not only did I need to rely more on Jesus, but I also needed to choose to be much more intentional with my time. Sitting in my sadness wasn't going to make things better. While it was good and even necessary for me to work through my feelings of disappointment, it was equally important for me to pick myself up and choose to take positive steps forward. Especially if I wanted to make the most of my time in this new place and new season.

I determined at that point to start setting goals. I recognized that I needed to steer the direction of my time and signal the intention for my time. My new season of life was not providing me with a clear set of instructions. Instead, it was more like I was being handed a pen and a blank sheet of paper titled "Morgan's Life."

As I previously mentioned, I still had a purpose in mothering and in my marriage, but beyond that my former life was just that—former. I had a clean slate in front of me. This was exciting and overwhelming all at the same time.

Before this season of life, I had been what you might call a casual goal setter and somewhat of a goal getter. I thought about the things I wanted to accomplish and eventually got around to doing some of them, some of the time. However, I wasn't looking at the year ahead with a big-picture mindset or choosing to break down my plans into short-term, medium-term, and long-term goals. I wasn't looking at each week and considering what I could do to better achieve the dreams and goals I was passionate about. I had an organic approach to goal setting, which can be limiting. I was not intentional, and therefore I was not charting a course for my time. By taking a casual approach to my goal setting, I was at best experiencing casual results.

When we do not set goals, the natural result is that we don't have a clear checks-and-balances system in place to help us with our time-management choices. Without defining our intentions for our time, we all too easily spend our time on things that don't align with what we want to experience and accomplish over the course of a day, week, month, or year.

In *Master Your Time, Master Your Life*, Brian Tracy writes:

> The biggest single waste of time is setting off without clear, specific goals. Many people waste their most productive years responding and reacting to whatever is going on around them and working to achieve the goals of other people instead of taking the time to become absolutely clear about what it is that they really want for themselves.
>
> There is a saying: "Before you do anything, you have to do something else first."
>
> Before you set off on the great adventure of life, you have to decide where you want to end up. The good news is there have never been more opportunities to achieve your goals than there are today. But only you can decide what you want.[1]

Setting goals and then working to achieve those goals will make the difference between a meaningful month or a meaningless month. When we set a goal and then meet it, it's like giving ourselves a big pat on the back and saying, "Great job!" (We all need more of this.)

Deciding to be more intentional about goal setting resulted in my time overseas being very fruitful. I could easily have settled into a season of complacency, closed off and unwilling to stretch myself. Instead, with God's help and the encouragement of friends and family, I decided to dive into new challenges and opportunities. Making the decision to organize my goals helped me to take back my time.

I am going to get into the "how" of setting goals, but first I'm going to talk about the "heart" and the "help" behind your goal setting.

## Goal Giving (Heart)

Goals get a bad rap. We hear every January that we need to set resolutions and goals. People say they are going to eat less, exercise more, shop less, and save more. Advertising and marketing teams work overtime to promote all things fitness and organizational related. They know people are feeling the need to say goodbye to their holiday indulgences and, once again, press the restart button. (At least until the Valentine's Day candy makes an appearance.)

These are all good things and they may very well need to be listed as resolutions or goals, but this is not the way I want you to think about your goals. I don't want you to think about things from a position of shame or guilt. I want you to consider what you want to do with your life and with your time. How can you use your time in the most meaningful way to impact not only your own life but also the lives of others around you? Goals should be self-serving *and* other-serving. This is where the true blessing of achieving your goals will be realized.

If you desire to take better care of your health, then setting a goal to exercise regularly will naturally overflow in the felt benefit to your loved ones. When your health is a priority, you will have more energy and stamina and, as a result, experience fewer health issues. This is a gift not only to you but also to your entire family.

If you commit to studying more of God's Word and memorizing Scripture, then God's words will pop into your mind as you need them to share with others. Your time spent learning more about God's love and instruction will result in an outpouring from your heart to those in your life. Through your God-inspired kind and thoughtful words and deeds, you will have a more positive impact on those whom God has placed in your life.

If you finally sign up to play on that sports team you've always wanted to join, then you may find a new group of people who are desperate for your gift of encouragement. You may be just the person to show them a little slice of Jesus's love. Even if it is during a form of competition!

Consider the heart behind the goals you set for yourself. Ask yourself how your goals will benefit you and how they will benefit others. How will setting goals help you to maximize your time? How is God wanting to stretch and grow you so that you have even more to offer?

Your goals should exist to inwardly serve you and outwardly serve others. Let your goals exist to help you become even more of a goal getter and a goal giver!

## Goal Cheering (Help)

One of the main reasons I have been successful with reaching my goals is because I have deliberately sought out accountability. When I find others who are committed to cheering me on, specifically when it comes to my goals,

I'm much more likely to stay the course. Cheerleaders are essential if we want to live intentionally.

When my friend Jill asked me to join her book club, I was all in. I had always wanted to be in a book club. Through the club I was introduced to the website Goodreads. The site provides a place to list books you want to read, are currently reading, and have finished reading. For someone who likes lists and tracking tools, this was a gift! I also discovered that I could set up an annual reading challenge for myself. Sign me up! (I think Jill's reading challenge was something like seventy-five books! Impressive, right?) Seeing her goal encouraged me, and I decided to set a goal to read twenty-five books that year. Having the reading challenge not only helped to motivate me to read and learn more, but being involved in the book club also gave me another layer of accountability and introduced me to books I might never have considered reading. In rediscovering my love for reading, I committed to doing different book studies with different friends and to leading a small group study. Jill was, and remains, my inspiration to keep reading, learning, and growing.

When I casually mentioned to my friend Cristina that I was thinking of signing up to run a full marathon (it was listed as one of my goals for that year), she told me that she would do it with me. I immediately thought to myself, *Why did I just open my mouth? Now I'm committed!*

Cristina's partnership and words of encouragement were just what I needed in order to fully commit. When you know someone is counting on you, it makes it easier to show up. On the day of the race, we met up, shivered in the chill of the early morning, made sure we had all of our necessities, and then took off. (For the record, I didn't bonk this time.) One steady step at a time, 26.2 miles to be exact, she and I made our way to the finish line. Crossing that line was the best feeling! After the race, I texted a picture to Cristina of my feet. I had to show her how bad they looked. They were covered with puffy water blisters, and I knew she would be able to truly appreciate my suffering. Later that day, she was the one who shared on my Facebook page: "It just dawned on me . . . YOU ARE A MARATHONER!!!! Way to go!" She was my cheerleader from start to finish and a big part of why I was able to accomplish my goal of running a marathon. I not only reached my goal but I also experienced the blessing of a closer friendship.

When we were struggling in our marriage, I set a goal to work on those things that I specifically needed to work on. I was definitely contributing to our problems. To help support me through this emotional time, I sought out mentors and friends who encouraged me and kept me focused. My friend Jena inspired me with her gentle words. She told me that God put David and me together and that we could grow through this and be stronger for it. She was also the one who told me to pack up for a week and take a trip back home to the Pacific Northwest. She said I needed time to recharge. Jena understood the challenges of living overseas, and she knew I was depleted emotionally, physically, mentally, and spiritually. My time for self-care was suffering. Her words were perfectly timed, and that week away was exactly what I needed in order to remain steadfast to my commitment to work on myself and my marriage.

Jena, Cristina, Jill, and many other amazing women have poured into my life. These women have used their gifts and time to support me. Their collective encouragement and cheerleading resulted in my ability to reach my goals. *Sometimes a positive word from someone is all we need in order to remain faithful.*

My mom sent me an email after she read the blog post I shared at the beginning of this chapter. She told me how hard it was for her to hear that I was going through such a challenging time. She ended her email to me by mentioning that maybe God was calling me to be a writer. Her words resonated and stuck with me. A small seed was planted, and now you are reading this book!

Her words were perfectly timed. I didn't know then what they might mean, but as I type these words today, I see the fruit.

If you want to live a life with increased purpose, cheerleaders are essential! Cheerleaders will help you achieve your goals. When you know someone is in your corner and that they have your back, it will give you the extra boost you need to keep going. Having the accountability of cheerleaders is the reason why I rediscovered my love for reading, committed to running 26.2 miles, and focused on my marriage relationship.

## Goal Setting (How)

Now I am going to share how to set goals. I want this part to be simple and something you can implement immediately. There is no need for perfection or overly complicated planning. Your intention is to create some tension that will help motivate you to maximize your time. As Hugh Culver says:

> When we create well-defined goals, whether they are to save more money, lose weight, increase our sales, or organize our office, we create new expectations and tension. The tension is between where we are now (our current reality) and where we want to go (our vision). This is a good thing! We need this tension to motivate us and to inspire us to overcome barriers and setbacks.[2]

To start planning your goals, refer back to chapter 2 and revisit what you listed as your purposes and priorities. The goals you set should align with your top purposes and priorities in your current season.

Consider your purposes and priorities and then ask God what he wants you to accomplish in your current season. Seek where he wants you to grow, how he wants you to bless others, and even what changes he wants you to make. God is a master cartographer; seek him as you work to map out your goals. Remember that the overarching objective is to be intentional with how you use your time, gifts, and talents. Your goals are like using your car blinker to signal changing lanes or taking a turn. They are signaling your intention.

My goal of wanting to read more was realized when I joined a book club. My season of life supported it as I had more available time to read. Before that season, I wasn't reading as much because my kids were younger and I was homeschooling them. I didn't have much free time, and it would have been nearly impossible for me to meet a goal of reading twenty-five books in a single year. That particular life season was not conducive to my involvement in a book club or setting a high reading challenge.

Likewise, running a marathon was something I was able to consider doing because my season supported it. I had not only the time but also the energy and motivation to properly train. Therefore, when Cristina came along, I was able to say yes to the opportunity, knowing that I could fully commit.

When we settled into our new season of living abroad, David and I recognized specific areas in our relationship we needed to address and improve on. This season helped to reveal what most needed our attention, and we intentionally chose to step up to the plate! This season helped return our focus to our relationship, which was and is one of our top priorities.

Your seasons will be a guiding force too, helping you to know what you can and cannot commit to. I was able to achieve my three goals because my season allowed the time required. Your goals will require your time; therefore, make sure you have the time to invest in the goals you set. Different seasons will allow for different goals.

By no means do I want you to simply settle in your current season or lay down things you believe at your core you are supposed to be doing. What I am saying is that when you are realistic about the amount of time you have available to work on your goals, this allows you to set and achieve realistic goals. Realistic goals mean you will be able to realize realistic results!

Yes, you may have to set down some of your goals for now. But remember, you won't have to tuck them away forever. There is a time for everything.

### The LIGHT Method

When setting goals, it is important to set them into specific categories and measurable time frames. Also, consider who will hold you accountable and how you will measure your success.

To help you with making a good plan for each of your goals, I'm going to introduce you to the LIGHT method. Just as you turn your signal light on when you are about to change lanes or turn right or left, you can use the LIGHT method to signal your intention, or the goal you want to accomplish. Or think of your goals as lighting the path you desire to take. Just as the traffic light tells you when to stop or go, the LIGHT method will help direct your steps as you work to meet your goals.

Though you don't necessarily need to complete a step-by-step guide for each and every goal you set, you will want to consider the principles of the LIGHT method for every goal. Just as you check your side mirrors, use your rearview mirror, and look straight ahead at the road in front of you, the LIGHT method will help you to look around before making your next move. This five-step method is a way to guarantee success!

*L is for List*. First, decide how and where you will list your goals. Like finding a calendar system that works for you, you want to find a method for listing your goals that works for you. This is a system you will refer to often; it should be posted somewhere visible. Seeing your plans displayed will remind you of what you want to work on week in and week out.

The total number of goals you set is up to you. Remember to work within your life season, intentionally listing goals that align best with your time and energies, and to factor in your personal design.

I recommend that at a minimum you sit down once a year, look ahead at the next twelve months, and consider what you want to do with your year. This could be January through December or fall through summer. Whatever method you choose, be consistent with your planning.

David and I have been setting family and marriage goals every fall for many years. I love looking back each year at what we listed as our top ten highlights for the previous year and then ahead to what ten things we want to do in the coming year. It is a simple tool that allows us to look backward and forward and also encourages us to be more intentional as both parents and spouses.

Rather than have one long list for all of your goals, divide them into separate lists corresponding to specific areas of your life. Revisit the purposes and priorities you listed in chapter 2. In my current season, I listed my goals in categories that align with my purposes: home, work, relationships, volunteering, and personal.

*I is for Intention.* Next, it is important to state your intention (goal) in a specific way. For example, if you work in sales, the goal "increase my sales and book more clients" is too vague. Instead, clarify your goal by stating *what* and *how*. Then determine the clear-cut steps required to meet your goal. Doing so will help you to better focus your time and energy. For example, *what* and *how* might be as follows:

What: "I want to acquire three new clients a
       month."

How: "I will add one additional form of advertising
      each month and seek referrals and reviews
      from my past clients."

Stating your goal in this way gives you a definitive direction. You now know what you need to *do* in order to increase your sales and book more clients.

*G is for Gauge.* When setting goals, you must consider how you will measure whether you have reached them. In the above example, a monthly log in which you list each additionally booked client would give you a fixed number and a clear result.

Or if your goal is to exercise more, setting a weekly goal with the number of times per week you will work out will help you to measure your success. A set number will give you something specific by which to determine whether you have reached your goal.

Don't be too rigid with your criterion. It is fine to adjust and tweak your benchmarks. The important piece is that you have something tangible to look at.

*H is for Help.* Enlist cheerleaders to hold you accountable. Tell others what you hope to achieve in the weeks and months ahead. Without others cheering you on, it will be more difficult for you to meet your goals. Find those who will support you, and look for those who want the very best for you. Seek those people in your life who will not only hold you accountable but also be your cheerleader. Don't be shy; share your goals with others. The more you talk about what you are working on, the more support you will enlist.

*T is for Time.* Lastly, set clear time frames for your goals in varying lengths of time: short-term (monthly), medium-term (quarterly), and long-term (annually). Designating a start and stop time for your goals will provide clear boundaries.

Also, with each goal you set, it is helpful to recognize what time zone it fits within. This will be beneficial as you plan and schedule. Different goals will naturally fall under different time zones. Knowing which time zone to assign to your goals will help to maximize your results. If you are working on learning how to knit, for example, you are not going to want to practice knitting while sitting on the bleachers watching a high school basketball game.

Using your time zones to balance the time you spend working on your goals will make a difference in what you are able to accomplish.

Following is an example of one of my goals using the LIGHT method:

**LIGHT**

**L**ist

**I**ntention

**G**auge

**H**elp

**T**ime

| List: | Take a class and learn how to knit.<br>(Purpose: Personal—hobby) |
|---|---|
| Intention: | Enroll in a six-week knitting class and purchase necessary supplies. |
| Gauge: | Successfully knit one scarf. |
| Help: | Ask my friend who knits for help when I have questions. |
| Time: | Medium-term—in three months I should have a new scarf. |
| Zone: | This is a GTZ activity for me because I am a beginner. |

## *Simplicity*

Often, we don't reach our goals because we don't create the time required to work on them. We think about our goals and our dreams, but we don't plan the time and space required to fulfill them. Successful goal setting and goal getting require a plan. You must signal in advance the changes you want to make. If you want to turn left, you need to signal accordingly. Signaling is an intention that you will change something. It tells others what you plan to do next.

Keep it simple and do what you plan to do. Don't be that person with their right blinker stuck on and neither changing lanes nor turning. And don't be that person who doesn't use their blinker but continues to change lanes and turn this way and that without communicating their intention and with no consistent plan.

*Look ahead, signal your intention, and then commit.*

Guess what? It is more than OK to remove a goal from your list. I do this often. I set goals for myself but then sometimes feel differently when push comes to shove and I'm on the other side, now having to execute what I previously thought was a good idea.

One year, one of my goals was to learn how to knit. As my Portuguese was limited and I had barely mastered ordering a drink at Starbucks, I chose not to sign up for a class. Instead, my kids and I set up YouTube videos, and we actively worked on guiding our knitting needles and following the step-by-step instructions. (This also turned out to be a gift as we all loved discovering a new hobby together.) That year, I was able to successfully knit one entire multicolored scarf. I was a knitter! I told myself, *Next year, I'm going to make another one, a better one!*

But you know what? I never got around to knitting anything else. Probably because I did not wear the first scarf I made and, I'll be honest, knitting is not easy. I realized at the end of the year that though continuing to knit had sounded like a good idea, it wasn't something I was passionate about. I had listed it merely as a next logical step rather than checking in with myself to determine if I truly desired to become a more skilled knitter.

It is fine to change course on the road of goal setting. Once you are on that road, you inevitably see your goals in a new light. Feel free to remove any that no longer "fit" (even if you haven't accomplished them). Every intention you list doesn't need to be fulfilled. Give yourself grace.

Change lanes or turn around when you need to, but just be sure to always keep your eyes on the road!

Ladies, I want you to keep things simple and take back your time. You have a limited amount of time, and I don't want you to limit what you can do with your time. Adopt a mindset of simply taking one step at a time, putting one foot in front of the other, twenty-four hours at a time, and diligently moving forward.

Set, plan, and steadily work to achieve your goals. As Rachel Hollis shares in *Girl, Wash Your Face*: "You have to shout out your hopes and dreams like the Great Bambino calling his shot. You need the courage to stand up and say, *'This one, right here: this is mine!'*"[3]

Then give God the eternal outcome and enjoy the immediate results of a job well done on this side of heaven. Fill your bucket list, set goals you are passionate about, and use your time to fulfill your highest and most important callings.

Keep your three time zones as the foundation and guardrails for making the most of your time. Let them be the heartbeat of your schedule and help you experience more harmony and less hustle.

Don't overthink implementing the zones; instead, as you go through your day, occasionally consider whether you are working in the correct zone at the correct time. Find the sweet spot between living in the moment and planning every moment. Avoid the trap of comparison, keep a big-picture mindset, and carefully choose between the things that drain you and those that fill you.

With every choice you make, seek to make the best choice. Don't settle for good or better—hold out for the best. The best choice for you will be the best way to invest your time. Ann Voskamp says, "You have only one decision every day: how will you use your time?"[4] Live with a twenty-four-hour perspective, and diligently carry the baton for the season you are in. This season, like other seasons, will come and go. Soak up the limited time you have right now, and remember that your time is a gift.

*Now is the time to take back your time!*

### ☼ Tip—Commit to a Goal Contract

▶ I will make time to plan and list my goals.

▶ I will commit to seeking support from my family and friends.

▶ I will carefully set attainable goals, considering the season of my life.

▶ I understand that it is OK to change my goals, adjust them, and even cross goals off my list.

▶ I understand that I am responsible for reaching my goals and that what I do day to day, month to month, and season to season will impact what I am able to achieve.

▶ I understand that oftentimes I may not feel like working on my goals, but I will work on them anyway. I will press forward and persevere.

► I understand that fear may keep me from reaching my goals, but I will not let fear stop me!

> Take back your time—
> signal where you want to go
> and don't forget
> to enjoy the ride!

# Conclusion

You can't make up for lost time. You can only do better
in the future.

Ashley Ormon

**A**s you hop back into the driver's seat and map out
your time in your current season of life, I want you
to promise me three things.

*Promise me that you will commit to being intentional while
also giving yourself much grace.*

A good friend of ours once said to me, in his Tennes-
seean Southern drawl, "Morgan, the laundry will be there
tomorrow." It's a simple truth and an important reminder.
While you want to make the most of your time today, you
don't want to stretch yourself so thin that you err on the
side of busyness or meaninglessness. Setting things down,
saying no, or even changing your mind are all part of being

a good time manager. Embrace your season, your productivity, and your design. When you understand who you are, you can be the best version of yourself, remain intentional, and enjoy a full life.

*Promise me that you will diligently apply the three time zones to your schedule.*

Whether you adopt a weekly view, daily view, task view, or your own unique view of scheduling the three time zones, be determined to consider what zone you are in within the blocks of time in your day. If I were to call you on the phone, I would love to hear you share that your morning was spent at the office in your YTZ or you enjoyed lunch with a close friend in your RTZ or your late afternoon required two hours in your GTZ to complete several time-sensitive to-dos. The more you stay in the applicable time zone for your priorities, the more productive you will be, whether you need to *focus*, *flex*, or *fill*! Be adaptable with the zones, and use them as a guide for your time. They will help you to steer in the best direction.

*Promise me that you will choose well, plan well, and live well.*

I hope you will seek fullness in every area of your life. Your time is a *responsibility*, a *privilege*, and a *gift*. Please do not settle for mediocrity. Every day you get a fresh twenty-four hours to take steps forward. One small step at a time can lead to big accomplishments over time. Be patient and purposeful. God has a wonderful plan for your life. Keep setting goals and working to find the sweet spot. Stay in your own lane, keep your eyes on the road in front of you, and *take back your time*!

I'm praying for you!

*Love,*
*Morgan*

# Notes

## Chapter 1 Your Time

1. Peter Walsh, *It's All Too Much: An Easy Plan for Living a Richer Life with Less Stuff* (New York: Free Press, 2007), 2.

2. Mary MacVean, "For Many People, Gathering Possessions Is Just the Stuff of Life," *Los Angeles Times*, March 21, 2014, http://articles.latimes.com/2014/mar/21/health/la-he-keeping-stuff-20140322.

3. Eric Carlson, "Trending Alert: 6 Reasons Why the Self Storage Industry Is on the Rise," *Life Storage* (blog), August 17, 2016, https://www.lifestorage.com/blog/storage/self-storage-industry-trends/.

4. Andy Stanley, *The Principle of the Path: How to Get from Where You Are to Where You Want to Be* (Nashville: Thomas Nelson, 2008), 14.

## Chapter 3 Your Productivity

1. Guy Kawasaki, LinkedIn, March 24, 2014, https://www.linkedin.com/pulse/20140324113914-2484700-let-s-stop-the-glorification-of-busy/.

2. Rory Vaden, *Procrastinate on Purpose: 5 Permissions to Multiply Your Time* (New York: Penguin Group, 2015), 8–9.

3. Lysa TerKeurst, *The Best Yes: Making Wise Decisions in the Midst of Endless Demands* (Nashville: Thomas Nelson, 2014), 229.

## Chapter 4 Your Green Time Zone (GTZ)

1. Dictionary.com, s.v. "moxie," accessed June 10, 2016, http://www.dictionary.com/browse/moxie?s=t.

## Chapter 5  Your Yellow Time Zone (YTZ)

1. *Sweet Home Alabama*, directed by Andy Tennant (Burbank, CA: Touchstone Pictures, 2002).

2. Quoted by Ryan Gromfin, The Restaurant Boss, accessed November 5, 2017, https://therestaurantboss.com/multitasking-steve-uzzell/.

3. Shauna Niequist, *Bittersweet: Thoughts on Change, Grace, and Learning the Hard Way* (Grand Rapids: Zondervan, 2010), 53.

## Chapter 6  Your Red Time Zone (RTZ)

1. Kory Kogon, Adam Merrill, and Leena Rinne, *The 5 Choices: The Path to Extraordinary Productivity* (New York: Simon & Schuster, 2016), 162–63, emphasis original.

2. Gale Bernhardt, "Everything You Need to Know about Bonking," Active, accessed December 15, 2017, https://www.active.com/triathlon/articles/everything-you-need-to-know-about-bonking.

3. Laura Vanderkam, *I Know How She Does It: How Successful Women Make the Most of Their Time* (New York: Penguin, 2017), 199.

4. Sarah Young, *Jesus Calling: Enjoying Peace in His Presence* (Nashville: Thomas Nelson, 2004), 311.

## Chapter 7  Your Design

1. Ann Voskamp, *The Broken Way: A Daring Path into the Abundant Life* (Grand Rapids: Zondervan, 2016), 59.

2. Tom Rath, *Strengths Finder 2.0* (New York: Gallup Press, 2007), ii–iii, emphasis original.

3. Carson Tate, *Work Simply: Embracing the Power of Your Personal Productivity Style* (New York: Penguin, 2015), 14.

4. Wikipedia, s.v. "Extraversion and introversion," last edited November 9, 2018, https://en.wikipedia.org/wiki/Extraversion_and_introversion.

## Chapter 8  Your Calendar

1. Tom Nikl, "How Many Employees Work at Disneyland on a Typical Day?," Quora, April 30, 2016, https://www.quora.com/How-many-employees-work-at-Disneyland-on-a-typical-day.

2. Micah Maddox, *Anchored In: Experience a Power-Full Life in a Problem-Filled World* (Nashville: Abingdon, 2017), 182–83.

3. Wikipedia, s.v. "Sweet spot (sports)," last edited August 7, 2018, https://en.wikipedia.org/wiki/Sweet_spot_(sports).

## Chapter 9 Your Goals

1. Brian Tracy, *Master Your Time, Master Your Life: The Breakthrough System to Get More Results, Faster, in Every Area of Your Life* (New York: Penguin, 2017), 11.

2. Hugh Culver, *Give Me a Break: The Art of Making Time Work for You* (Canada: Kaire Publishing, 2011), 60.

3. Rachel Hollis, *Girl, Wash Your Face: Stop Believing the Lies About Who You Are So You Can Become Who You Were Meant to Be* (Nashville: Thomas Nelson, 2018), 60, emphasis added.

4. Voskamp, *The Broken Way*, 59.

**Morgan Tyree** is a professional organizer (chaos calmer), writer (list lover), and fitness instructor (exercise enthusiast). She has a desire to help women be their best and to encourage and equip them in every season of life by inspiring intentionality. She earned her BS degree in business administration with an emphasis in small business and entrepreneurship from the University of Oregon and has worked in the fields of marketing, management, and human resources. She runs her own personal organization and time-management business and lives with her husband, David, and their three children (affectionately termed their ABCs) in Colorado. Morgan invites you to join her on a peaceful path to simplicity. Connect with her online at morganizewithme.com.

# Learn to Entertain with
# Joy *and* Confidence

Does the thought of hosting a dinner send you into spasms of delight or spirals of dismay? With personal assessments, encouraging stories, and plenty of practical ideas, Morgan Tyree shows you how to identify and embrace your hospitality personality so you can stop worrying and start enjoying!

*Connect with*
# Morgan

# MorganizeWithMe.com

Visit Morgan online to shop her selection of products and
downloadable resources. Subscribe to her email list to
receive free updates, tips on organizing, and much more!

 MorganizeWithMe       MorganizeWithMe

 MorganizeWithMe       morgantyree